Key Performance Indicators

Key Performance Indicators

Developing, Implementing, and Using Winning KPIs

DAVID PARMENTER

John Wiley & Sons, Inc.

Library of Congress Cataloging-in-Publication Data:

Parmenter, David.
    Key performance indicators : developing, implementing, and using
winning KPIs / David Parmenter.
        p.   cm.
    Includes index.
    ISBN-13: 978-0-470-09588-1 (cloth)
    ISBN-10: 0-470-09588-1 (cloth)
    1. Performance technology.   2. Performance standards.
    3. Organizational effectiveness.   I. Title.
  HF5549.5.P37P37   2007
  658.40'13— dc22   2006020849

Printed in the United States of America

10 9 8 7 6

CONTENTS

Contents

PREFACE

This book is aimed at providing the missing link between the balanced scorecard work of Kaplan and Norton[1] and the reality of implementing performance measurement in an organization. The implementation difficulties were first grasped by a KPI manual developed by AusIndustry as part of a "portfolio" of resources for organizations pursuing international best practices. This book has adopted many of the approaches of the KPI manual, which was first published in 1996, and has incorporated more implementation tools, the balanced scorecard philosophy, the author's work on "winning key performance indicators" (KPIs), and many checklists to assist with implementation.

EMBARKING ON A KPI/BALANCED SCORECARD PROJECT

The goal of this book is to help minimize the risks that working on a KPI/balanced scorecard project encompasses. It is designed for the project team, senior management, external project facilitators, and team coordinators whose role it is to steer such a project to success. The role they play could leave a great legacy in the organization for years to come, or could amount to nothing by joining the many performance measurement initiatives that have failed. It is my wish that the material in this book, along with the workshops I deliver around the world, will increase the likelihood of success.

In order for both you and your project to succeed, I suggest that you:

- Read Chapters 1 and 2 carefully, a couple of times.

- Visit my Web site www.waymark.co.nz for other useful information.

- Scan the material in the subsequent chapters so you know what is there.

- Begin Step 1 in Chapter 3 by setting up the focus group one-day workshop.

- Seek an outside facilitator, who will help guide/mentor you in the early weeks of the project.

- Commence the project team-building exercises and undertake any training to plug those identified skill gaps in the project team.

How to Use This Book

Due to the common misunderstandings that exist in relation to KPIs, it is important that all project team members, management, and staff are aware of the structure and content of this guide.

Using Chapter 1: Introduction

For years organizations that have had what they thought were KPIs have not had the focus, adaptability, innovation, and profitability that they were seeking. KPIs themselves were mislabeled and misused. Examine a company with over 20 KPIs and you will find a lack of focus, lack of alignment, and underachievement. Some organizations try to manage with over 40 KPIs, many of which are not actually KPIs. This chapter explains a new way of breaking performance measures

	Overview	Target Audience
Chapter 1	Background. Draws on the latest theory as to differences between key result indicators (KRIs), performance indicators (PIs), and KPIs.	All members of the KPI team, the external project facilitator, team coordinators, local project facilitators, senior management, and board members will need to read this chapter to fully understand what KRIs, PIs, and KPIs are.
Chapter 2	The foundation stones for implementing KPIs. Discusses the four principles that need to be applied.	All members of the KPI team, the external project facilitator, team coordinators, local project facilitators, and the senior management team will need to read this chapter to fully understand the importance of these foundation stones.
Chapter 3	A 12-step model for developing and using KPIs. It is important that this chapter is fully understood before commencing the project.	KPI team, the external project facilitator, team coordinators, local project facilitators, and individual team members who will be responsible for the development of PIs and KPIs.
Chapter 4	The KPI team's resource kit including work-sheets, workshop programs, and questionnaires.	KPI team, the external project facilitator, team coordinators, and local project facilitators, who will be undertaking the various exercises.
Chapter 5	Templates for reporting performance measures (including KRIs, PIs, and KPIs).	The project team, reporting accountants, and the senior management team. This chapter saves time by utilizing better-practice reporting templates.
Chapter 6	External project facilitator's resource kit.	The project team, senior management, and the external facilitator.
Appendix	List of performance measures (including KRIs, PIs and KPIs) to assist with the short-listing of likely performance measures.	KPI team, the external project facilitator, team coordinators, and local project facilitators, who will be overseeing the implementation.

into key result indicators, performance indicators, and key performance indicators. It also explains a significant shift in the way KPIs are used to ensure they do not create dysfunctional behavior.

Using Chapter 2: Foundation Stones for Implementing Key Performance Indicators

Effective organizational change is heavily reliant on creating appropriate people practices as the centerpiece of a new workplace culture. In this context, the introduction of KPIs must be achieved in a way that supports and extends the idea of a cooperative partnership in the workplace — a partnership among employees, management, suppliers, customers, and the communities in which the organization operates. This chapter advances four general principles, called the four foundation stones:

1. Partnership with the staff, unions, key suppliers, and key customers

2. Transfer of power to the front line

3. Integration of measurement, reporting, and improvement of performance

4. Linkage of performance measures to strategy

Using Chapter 3: Developing and Using KPIs: A 12-Step Model

When you are ready to introduce performance measures (including result indicators, performance indicators, and KPIs) into your organization, we anticipate that you will want to broadly follow the 12-step approach outlined in this chapter. This chapter analyzes each step, its purpose, how it relates to the four foundation stones, guidelines on how to use it, and a checklist to ensure that the key steps are undertaken.

Using Chapter 4: KPI Team Resource Kit

This chapter provides the KPI team with useful tools for gathering information. For many of the steps, a questionnaire has been included and, in some cases, a worksheet that needs to be completed by the project team or by the teams developing their performance measures. For all key workshop sessions, a program has been developed based on successful ones run by the author.

Using Chapter 5: Templates for Reporting Performance Measures

This chapter illustrates how to present KRIs, PIs, and KPIs. Electronic templates can be acquired from www.waymark.co.nz (for a small fee). Readers who provide additional formats to KPIformats@ waymark.co.nz that are not already on the website will be able to get a discount on this fee providing Waymark Solutions decides to use them and are given the right to publish them.

Using Chapter 6: Facilitator's Resource Kit

The process for developing and using performance measures (including KRIs, PIs, and KPIs) is assisted by the involvement of a skilled KPI facilitator sourced from outside the company. The facilitator's key roles are to help educate the senior management team, set up the project team, and then mentor the project team. Chapter 3 suggests that certain key activities within the 12 steps should be performed by this external facilitator.

Using the Appendix: Performance Measures Database

The appendix provides a list of performance measures (including KRIs, PIs, and KPIs), some of which will be relevant for your organization. These are organized according to balanced scorecard perspectives and are constantly being updated. Updated versions are available via www.waymark.co.nz (for a small fee). Readers who contribute additional measures to KPImeasures@waymark.co.nz will be rewarded with a discount on this fee.

The manual is a resource for anyone in the organization involved with the development and use of KPIs. It is desirable that all KPI project team members, the external project facilitator, team coordinators, and local facilitators (if required) have their own manual to ensure all follow the same plan. Team members are expected to take the manual with them when meeting staff and management, as they will be able to clarify issues by using examples from the manual. However, note that this manual is copyrighted, so it is a breach of the copyright to photocopy sections for distribution.

Endnote

1. Robert S. Kaplan and David P. Norton, *The Balanced Scorecard: Translating Strategy into Action.* Boston: Harvard Business School Press, 1996.

ACKNOWLEDGMENTS

I would like to acknowledge the commitment and dedication of Waymark Solutions staff over the years this project has taken (Sean, Dean, Jacqueline, Roydon); Debbie Parker, who read through the early drafts; Nadra, Alexandra, and Claudine who have had to put up with my many late nights at the office and finally all those who have attended my KPI workshops and shared their ideas on "winning KPIs."

Key Performance Indicators

CHAPTER 1

Introduction

Many companies are working with the wrong measures, many of which are incorrectly termed key performance indicators (KPIs). Very few organizations really monitor their true KPIs. The reason is that very few organizations, business leaders, writers, accountants, and consultants have explored what a KPI actually is. There are three types of performance measures (see Exhibit 1.1):

1. Key result indicators (KRIs) tell you how you have done in a perspective.
2. Performance indicators (PIs) tell you what to do.
3. KPIs tell you what to do to increase performance dramatically.

Many performance measures used by organizations are thus an inappropriate mix of these three types.

An onion analogy can be used to describe the relationship of these three measures. The outside skin describes the overall condition of the onion, the amount of sun, water, and nutrients it has received; how it has been handled from harvest to supermarket shelf. However, as we peel the layers off the onion, we find more information. The layers represent the various performance indicators, and the core, the key performance indicators.

Exhibit 1.1 Three Types of Performance Measures

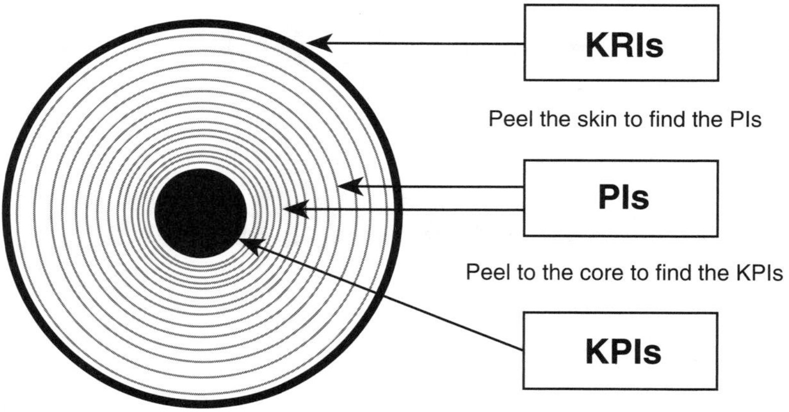

KEY RESULT INDICATORS

What are *KRIs*? KRIs are measures that have often been mistaken for KPIs, including:

- Customer satisfaction
- Net profit before tax
- Profitability of customers
- Employee satisfaction
- Return on capital employed

The common characteristic of these measures is that they are the result of many actions. They give a clear picture of whether you are traveling in the right direction. They do not, however, tell you what you need to do to improve these results. Thus, KRIs provide information that is ideal for the board (i.e., those not involved in day-to-day management).

A car's speedometer provides a useful analogy. The board will simply want to know the speed the car is traveling. However, management needs to know more information since the traveling speed is a combination of what gear the car is in and the revolutions per minute (RPMs) of the engine. Management might even be concentrating on completely different measures, such as how economically the car is performing (miles per gallon), or how hot the engine is running. These are two completely different gauges and are performance indicators or might even be KPIs.

KRIs typically cover a longer period of time than KPIs; they are reviewed on monthly/quarterly cycles, not on a daily/weekly basis as KPIs are. Separating KRIs from other measures has a profound impact on reporting, resulting in a separation of performance measures into those impacting governance and those impacting management. That is, an organization should have a governance report (ideally in a dashboard format), consisting of up to ten measures providing high-level KRIs for the board and a balanced scorecard (BSC) comprising up to 20 measures (a mix of KPIs and PIs) for management.

In between KRIs and the true KPIs are numerous performance indicators. These complement the KPIs and are shown with them on the scorecard for the organization and the scorecard for each division, department, and team.

Performance indicators that lie beneath KRIs could include:

- Profitability of the top 10% of customers
- Net profit on key product lines
- Percentage increase in sales with top 10% of customers
- Number of employees participating in the suggestion scheme

KEY PERFORMANCE INDICATORS

What are *KPIs?*

KPIs represent a set of measures focusing on those aspects of organizational performance that are the most critical for the current and future success of the organization.

KPIs are rarely new to the organization. They have either not been recognized or were "gathering dust" somewhere unknown to the current management team. KPIs can be illustrated by two examples:

Example: An Airline KPI

This example concerns a senior BA official, who set about turning British Airways (BA) around in the 1980s by reportedly concentrating on one KPI. He was notified, wherever he was in the world, if a BA plane was delayed. The BA manager at the relevant airport knew that if a plane was delayed beyond a certain "threshold," they would receive a personal call from the BA official. It was not long before BA planes had a reputation for leaving on time. This KPI affected all six of the BSC perspectives. Late planes:

- Increased cost in many ways, including additional airport surcharges, and the cost of accommodating passengers overnight as a result of planes being "curfewed" due to noise restrictions late at night

- Increased customers' dissatisfaction, and alienation of those people meeting passengers at their destination (possible future customers)

- Contributed more to ozone depletion (environmental impact) as additional fuel was used in order to make up time during the flight

- Had a negative impact on staff development as they learned to replicate the bad habits that created late planes

- Adversely affected supplier relationships and servicing schedules resulting in poor service quality

- Increased employee dissatisfaction, as they were constantly "firefighting" and dealing with frustrated customers

Example: A Distribution Company

A CEO of a distribution company realized that a critical success factor for their business was trucks leaving as close to capacity as possible. A large train truck capable of carrying more than 40 tons was being sent out with small loads as dispatch managers were focusing on "delivering in full on time" to customers.

Each day by 9 A.M., the CEO received a report of those trailers that had been sent out underweight. The CEO called the dispatch manager and asked whether any action had taken place to see if the customer could have accepted the delivery on a different date that would enable better utilization of the trucks. In most cases the customer could have received it earlier or later, fitting in with a past or future truck going in that direction. The impact on profitability was significant.

Just with the airline example, staff did their utmost to avoid a career-limiting phone call with their CEO!

Seven Characteristics

From extensive analysis and from discussions with over 1,500 participants in my KPI workshops, covering most organization types in the public and private sectors, I define seven KPI characteristics:

1. Nonfinancial measures (not expressed in dollars, yen, pounds, euros, etc.)
2. Measured frequently (e.g., daily or 24/7)
3. Acted on by the CEO and senior management team
4. Understanding of the measure and the corrective action required by all staff
5. Ties responsibility to the individual or team
6. Significant impact (e.g., affects most of the core critical success factors [CSFs] and more than one BSC perspective)
7. Positive impact (e.g., affects all other performance measures in a positive way)

When you put a dollar sign on a measure, you have already converted it into a result indicator (e.g., daily sales are a result of activities that have taken place to create the sales). The KPI lies deeper down. It may be the number of visits to contacts with the key customers who make up most of the profitable business.

KPIs should be monitored 24/7, daily, or perhaps weekly for some. A monthly, quarterly, or annual measure cannot be a KPI, as it cannot be *key* to your business if you are monitoring it well after the "horse has bolted." KPIs are therefore "current-" or future-oriented measures as opposed to past measures (e.g., number of key customer visits planned in next month or a list by key customer of the date of the next planned visit). When you look at most organizational measures, they are very much past indicators measuring events of the last month or quarter. These indicators cannot be and never were KPIs.

All good KPIs make a difference; they have the CEO's constant attention, with daily calls to the relevant staff. Having a "career-limiting" discussion with the CEO is not something the staff wants to repeat, and in the airline case, innovative and productive processes were put in place to prevent a recurrence.

A KPI should tell you what action needs to take place. The British Airways "late plane" KPI communicated immediately to everyone that there needed to be a focus on recovering the lost time. Cleaners, caterers, ground crew, flight attendants, and liaison officers with traffic controllers would all work some magic to save a minute here and a minute there, while maintaining or improving service standards.

A KPI is deep enough in the organization that it can be tied to an individual. In other words, the CEO can call someone and ask "why." Return on capital employed has never been a KPI, as it cannot be tied to a manager—it is a result of many activities under different managers.

A good KPI will affect most of the core CSFs and more than one BSC perspective. In other words, when the CEO, management, and staff focus on the KPI, the organization scores goals in all directions.

A good KPI has a flow-on effect. An improvement in a key measure within the CSF of customer satisfaction would have a positive impact on many other measures. Timely arrival and departure of planes gives rise to improved service by ground staff, as there is less "firefighting" to distract them from a quality and caring customer contact.

Lead and Lag Confusion

Many management books that cover KPIs talk about "lead and lag indicators"; this merely clouds the KPI debate. Using the new way of looking at performance measures, we dispense with the terms *lag* (outcome) and *lead* (performance driver) indicators. At seminars, when the audience is asked "Are the late planes in the air KPI, a lead indicator, or a lag indicator?" The vote count is always evenly split. Surely, this is enough proof that *lead* and *lag* labels are not a useful way of defining performance measures.

KRIs replace outcome measures, which typically look at activity over months or quarters. PIs and KPIs are now characterized as either past-, current-, or future-focused measures. The new concept called *current measures* refers to those monitored 24/7 or daily, for example, sales made yesterday. You will find your KPIs in your organization are either current- or future-oriented measures.

In workshops I ask participants to write a couple of their major measures in the worksheet shown in Exhibit 1.2, and then restate the measure in the other tenses. Take time out now and restate three measures (see Exhibit 1.2).

The lead/lag division did not focus adequately enough on current or future-oriented measures. If quality improvements are to happen, the number of initiatives that are about to come online in the next week, two weeks, or month must be measured. If we want to increase sales, what is important to know is the number of meetings that have already been organized/scheduled with our key customers in the next week, two weeks, or month.

Exhibit 1.2 Past/Current/Future Performance Measures Analysis Worksheet

Past Measures	Current Measures	Future Measures
Last week/two weeks/ month/quarter	*24/7 and daily*	*Next day/week/month/ quarter*
For example, number of late planes last week/last month	For example, planes over two hours late (updated continuously)	For example, number of initiatives to be commenced in the next month/two months to target areas that are causing late planes

10/80/10 Rule

Kaplan and Norton recommend no more than 20 KPIs. Hope and Fraser[1] suggest fewer than 10 KPIs. The 10/80/10 rule is a good guide. That is, there are about 10 KRIs, up to 80 PIs, and 10 KPIs in an organization (see Exhibit 1.3). Very seldom are more measures needed, and in many cases even fewer.

For many organizations 80 PIs will at first appear totally inadequate. Yet on investigation, you will find that separate teams are actually working with variations of the same indicator, so it is better to standardize them (e.g., a "number of training days in the last month" performance measure should be consistently applied with the same definition graph).

Many KPI project teams will also, at first, feel that having only 10 KPIs is too restrictive and may wish to increase KPIs to 30. With careful analysis these will soon be reduced to the 10 suggested unless the organization is made up of many businesses from very different sectors, in which case the 10/80/10 rule can apply to each diverse business, providing it is large enough to warrant its own KPI rollout.

Importance of Timely Measurement

Before proceeding further, we will look at the importance of measurement. The use of measurement varies widely across the world.

Exhibit 1.3   10/80/10 Rule

Key result indicator (10)	Tells you how you have done in a perspective
Performance indicator (80)	Tells you what to do
Key performance indicator (10)	Tells you what to do to increase performance dramatically

In the United States, many businesses use the BSC to create behavioral alignment in a balanced way.

It is essential that measurement be timely. Today, a KPI provided to management that is in excess of five days old is useless. KPIs are prepared in real time, with even weekly ones available by the next working day. The suggested reporting framework of performance indicators is set out in Exhibit 1.4.

One or two KPIs should be updated daily or even 24/7 (as in the British Airways case).

Most organizations will have five essential KPIs, which must be reported weekly at least (excluding the daily or 24/7 KPIs identified above). Performance measures that focus on completion should be included. Projects that are running late and overdue reports should be reported to the senior management team each week. Such reporting will revolutionize project and task completion in your organization.

Exhibit 1.4   Suggested Reporting Framework

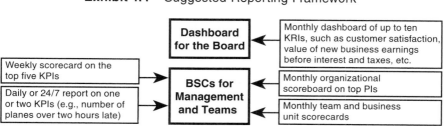

The remaining performance measures should be reported monthly and include a team and business unit BSC.

Learned Reaction to Measurement

Measurement initiatives are often viewed as managerial control devices and solely for the benefit of management. As a result, employees often tend to respond with distrust to the implementation of performance measurement in their workplace.

Measurement can become a source of division and conflict between managers and their employees. It can even result in adverse results wherein employees circumvent intended outcomes. A classic example is provided by a city train service that had an on-time measure with some draconian penalties. Train drivers who were behind schedule learned to simply stop at the top end of each station triggering the green light at the other end of the platform, and then carry on without opening the doors; the trains were then on time, but there were many unhappy customers both on the train and on the platform.

Such behavior suggests that a "better-practice" approach to performance measurement was not followed. There needs to be a new approach to measurement—one that is consultative, promotes partnership, and obtains behavioral alignment, empowering all the people who work in the organization.

MANAGEMENT MODELS THAT HAVE A PROFOUND IMPACT ON KPIs

Balanced Scorecard

The groundbreaking work of Kaplan and Norton[2] brought to management's attention that performance needed to be measured in a more holistic way. They came up with four perspectives that have been increased to six in this book. Kaplan and Norton's new work on strategic mapping[3] alludes to the importance of employee satisfaction and the environment/community perspectives. The latter is important because it means the BSC now incorporates all triple bottom-line issues (see Exhibit 1.5).

Beyond Budgeting Management Model

It is easy for the BSC, with its financial and non-financial measures, to develop into yet another fixed performance contract and eventually result in the same dysfunctional behavior that we see with the annual planning process.

The adoption of the beyond budgeting management model will enhance the power of the BSC. Companies worldwide are beginning to recognize that existing budget processes are not satisfactory. They have been used since the Romans planned and budgeted their invasion of northern Europe! The budget process is often seen as a hindrance to management rather than being beneficial. An international survey of chief financial officers (CFOs) in 1998 by the U.S. consulting firm Hackett Benchmarking & Research found that almost 90% of CFOs were dissatisfied with their budget process and that the

Exhibit 1.5 Six-Perspective Balanced Scorecard

FINANCIAL	CUSTOMER	ENVIRONMENT/ COMMUNITY
Utilization of assets, optimization of working capital	Increase customer satisfaction, targeting customers who generate the most profit	Supporting local businesses, linking with future employees, community leadership
INTERNAL	EMPLOYEE SATISFACTION	LEARNING AND GROWTH
Delivery in full on time, optimizing technology, effective relationships with key stakeholders	Positive company culture, retention of key staff, increased recognition	Empowerment, increasing expertise, and adaptability

annual budget was not linked to organizational strategy. KPIs are a step in the right direction.

Hope and Fraser,[4] the "management gurus" behind the "Beyond Budgeting Movement" have stated that not only is the budget process a time-consuming, costly exercise generating little value, but also, and more importantly, it becomes a major limiting factor on how your organization can perform. They provide examples of companies that have broken free from the budget constraint and achieved success well beyond expectations. Organizations that go beyond budgeting are empowering their frontline staff, the very thing that KPIs require. In other words, KPIs will be enhanced with the removal of the budget process.

Establishment of a quarterly rolling planning regime, wherein management both sets out their expenditure requirements for the next 18 months and seeks approval for expenditure planned for the next three months, is a key requirement (see Exhibit 1.6).

Converting Reporting from Information Memorandums to Decision-Based Reports

Many management reports are not management tools; they are merely memorandums of information. As a management tool, management reports should encourage timely action in the right direction. Organizations need to measure and report on those activities on which the board, management, and staff need to focus. The old adage "What gets measured gets done" is still true.

For management reporting to become a management tool, monthly reporting must be combined with daily and weekly reporting. It is of little help to tell the senior management team that "the horse has bolted" halfway through the following month. If management is told immediately "the stable door has been left open," most are soon able to "close" it.

This has a profound impact on the KPI reporting that needs to be timely, brief, and informative.

Exhibit 1.6 How Quarterly Rolling Planning Works for an Organization with a Year-End that Falls at the End of a Traditional Calendar Quarter

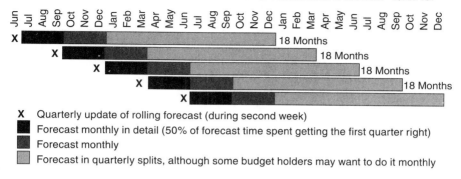

X Quarterly update of rolling forecast (during second week)

■ Forecast monthly in detail (50% of forecast time spent getting the first quarter right)

■ Forecast monthly

▨ Forecast in quarterly splits, although some budget holders may want to do it monthly

People Practices

At the center of all organizations are people practices—these are integral to all the elements of best practice. It is important that the KPI team understand them, as many KPIs and PIs will influence them.

The placement of people practices at the center of all organizations is deliberate. The ability of any organization to pursue the best-practice path to performance improvement is determined by the effectiveness of its people practices (see Exhibit 1.7).

Examples of people practices that leading firms adopt include:

- Effective, integrated top-down and bottom-up communications
- Self-managing teams
- Focus on, and measurement of, employee satisfaction
- Training and development processes that promote career paths (including mentorship programs, empowerment programs, leadership training, running in-house development centers, etc.)
- Excellent occupational health and safety practices
- Focus on internal (and external) customers
- Innovative staff recognition systems (including CEO success express, CEO bouquets)

Exhibit 1.7   People Practices

- Practical remuneration systems
- Migration away from the classical staff performance review cycle, which is cumbersome, expensive, and too late to be of any use

DEFINITIONS

The following definitions are listed in order of importance:

Performance measure. Throughout this manual, the term performance measure refers to an indicator used by management to measure, report, and improve performance. These are classed as either a key result indicator, a performance indicator, or a key performance indicator.

Balanced scorecard. A term first introduced by Kaplan and Norton describing how one needs to measure performance in a more holistic way. One needs to see an organization's performance in a number of different perspectives. For the purposes of this manual there are six perspectives in a balanced scorecard (see Exhibit 1.5).

Oracles and "top guns." Oracles in an organization are those gray-haired individuals who have seen it all before. They are often considered to be slow, ponderous, and, quite frankly, a nuisance by the new management. Often, they are retired early or made redundant only to be rehired as contractors at twice the previous salary when management realizes they have lost too much institutional knowledge. Their considered pace is often a reflection that they can see that an exercise is futile as it has failed twice before!

The "top guns" are young, fearless, and precocious leaders of the future who are not afraid to go where "angels fear to tread." These staff members have not yet achieved management positions.

The mixing of the oracles and young guns benefits both parties and the organization. The young guns learn much and the oracles rediscover their energy being around these live wires!

Empowerment. For the purposes of this book, *empowerment* is an outcome of a process that matches competencies, skills, and motivations with the required level of autonomy and responsibility in the workplace.

Senior management team (SMT). The senior management team is comprised of the CEO and all direct reports.

Better practice. This is the efficient and effective way management and staff undertake business activities in all key processes: leadership, planning, customers, suppliers, community relations, production and supply of products and services, employee well-being, and so forth.

Best practice. This is a commonly misused term, especially as what is best practice for one organization may not be best practice for another, albeit in the same sector. Best practice is where better practices, when effectively linked together, lead to sustainable "world-class" outcomes in quality, customer service, flexibility, timeliness, innovation, cost, and competitiveness.

Best-practice organizations commonly use the latest time-saving technologies, always focus on the 80/20, are members of quality management and continuous improvement professional bodies, and utilize benchmarking.

Exhibit 1.8 shows the contents of the toolkit used by best-practice organizations to achieve world-class performance.

Benchmarking. Benchmarking can be defined as an ongoing, systematic process to search for international better practices, compare against them, and then introduce them, modified where necessary, into your organization. Benchmarking may be focused on products, services, business practices, and processes of recognized leading organizations.

Exhibit 1.8 Best-Practice Toolkit

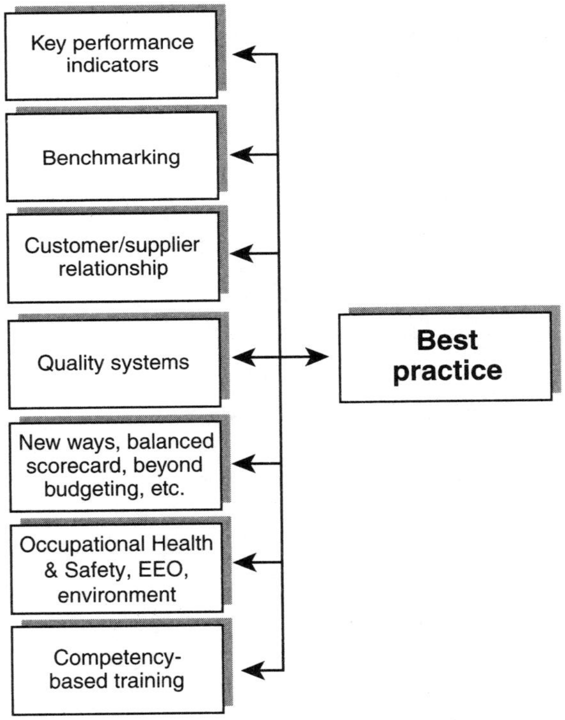

Endnotes

1. Jeremy Hope and Robin Fraser, *Beyond Budgeting: How Managers Can Break Free from the Annual Performance Trap.* Boston: Harvard Business School Press, 2003.

2. Robert S. Kaplan and David P. Norton, *The Balanced Scorecard: Translating Strategy into Action.* Boston: Harvard Business School Press, 1996.

3. Robert S. Kaplan and David P. Norton, *Strategy Maps: Converting Intangible Assets into Tangible Outcomes.* Boston: Harvard Business School Press, 2004.

4. See note 1 above.

CHAPTER 2

Foundation Stones for Implementing Key Performance Indicators

The ultimate success of a change strategy depends greatly on *how* the change is introduced and implemented, rather than on the merit of the strategy itself. Successful development and utilization of key performance indicators (KPIs) in the workplace is determined by the presence or absence of four foundation stones (see Exhibit 2.1):

1. Partnership with the staff, unions, key suppliers, and key customers

2. Transfer of power to the front line

3. Integration of measurement, reporting, and improvement of performance

4. Linkage of performance measures to strategy

Exhibit 2.1   Four Foundation Stones for KPI Development

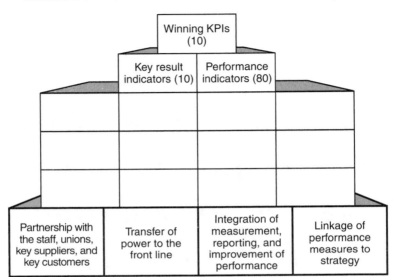

Exhibit 2.1   Four Foundation Stones for KPI Development

FOUR FOUNDATON STONES GUIDING THE DEVELOPMENT AND USE OF KPIs

Partnership Foundation Stone

The successful pursuit of performance improvement requires the establishment of an effective partnership between management, local employee representatives, unions representing the organization's employees, employees, major customers, and major suppliers. Implications of the partnership foundation stone include:

- Recognition by all stakeholders that significant organizational and cultural change requires a mutual understanding and acceptance of the need for change and how it is to be implemented
- Commitment to the establishment and maintenance of effective consultative arrangements with unions, employee representatives, and employees

- Joint development of a strategy for the introduction of best practice and KPIs
- Extension of the notion of partnership to include and involve the organization's key customers and key suppliers

Transfer of Power to the Frontline Foundation Stone

Successful performance improvement requires empowerment of the organization's employees, particularly those in the operational "front line."

Implications of the transfer of power to the frontline foundation stone include:

- The operation of effective top-down and bottom-up communication, including significant access to strategic organizational information
- The empowerment of employees to take immediate action to rectify situations that are negatively impacting KPIs (e.g., able to authorize doubling up of cleaning staff in order to speed up turnaround time for an anticipated late plane)
- Devolving responsibility to the teams to develop and select their own performance measures
- Provision of training on: empowerment, KPIs, the organization's critical success factors, and process improvement methods
- Additional support for those employees with literacy, numeracy, or other learning-related difficulties

Integration of Measurement, Reporting, and Improvement of Performance Foundation Stone

It is critical that management develop an integrated framework so that performance is measured and reported in a way that results in action. Organizations should be reporting events on a daily/weekly/monthly basis, depending on their significance, and these reports should cover the critical success factors (CSFs). The human resources (HR) team has an important role to ensure that the workforce perceives performance measurement in a positive way (e.g., a way to increase their long-term job satisfaction rather than the old views of performance measurement so well portrayed in the Peter Sellers film *I'm All Right Jack*—a must-see for all of the KPI team).

Implications of the measurement, reporting, and improvement of performance foundation stone include:

- The development of performance-improvement strategies and performance measures becomes an iterative process in time. That is, the direction and context for change progressively become modified and informed as teams are increasingly empowered and develop innovative solutions and ideas.

- There needs to be a major revamp of reporting so that it is more concise, timely, efficient to produce, and focused on decision making.

- Organizational performance measures will be modified in response to the performance measures developed at team level.

Linking Performance Measures to Strategy Foundation Stone

Performance measures are meaningless unless they are linked to the organization's current CSFs, the balanced scorecard (BSC) perspectives, and the organization's strategic objectives. Exhibit 2.2 shows the linkages clearly.

An organization will be more successful if it has spent time defining and conveying its vision, mission, and values. It needs to be defined in such a way that staff and management intuitively work with them on a daily basis. CEOs who are great leaders and motivators—they often go hand in hand—continually promote the virtues of these three "beacons."

Exhibit 2.2   Journey from a Mission and Vision to Performance Measures that Work

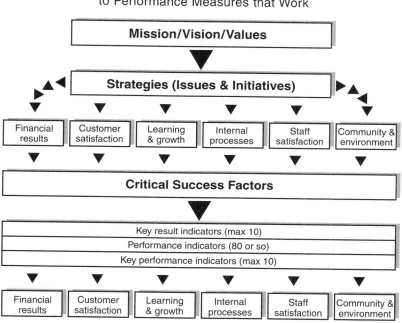

It is important that an organization has a well-considered and well-constructed strategy. These strategies need to link back to the six BSC perspectives. You may find when you cross-check your strategies to these perspectives that some perspectives might not be covered, in which case a revisit to the strategies may be required. Commonly, an organization can juggle only a few strategies at the same time, for example, less than five strategies at any one time. Naturally, these will change over time. Applications are now available that can assist greatly in formulating and deploying strategic direction. These applications often incorporate the BSC philosophy.

Ascertaining an organization's CSFs is a major exercise, and one that is often only obliquely tackled. CSFs identify the issues that determine an organization's health and vitality. When you first investigate CSFs, you may come up with 30 or so issues that can be argued are critical for the continued health of the organization. The second phase of thinning them down is easy, as the more important CSFs have a broader influence cutting across a number of BSC perspectives. Better practice suggests that there should be only between *five and eight* CSFs. Once you have the right CSFs, finding the KPIs is much easier, as they will reside within these CSFs.

The traditional scorecard needs modifying to encompass two areas particularly important to the HR team — staff satisfaction and environment/community perspectives. These were underestimated in the original groundbreaking work of Robert Kaplan and David Norton.[1] Having a separate employee satisfaction perspective emphasizes the importance of measuring the key drivers such as the amount and regularity of recognition (e.g., how many recognitions have been made this week, the past two weeks, this month). It will also support the need for more regular staff satisfaction surveys performed on a rolling sample basis.

The environment/community perspective will help create a major asset to the HR team, helping the organization become an employer of choice. Long-term successful linkages with the community, both local and national, are extremely valuable. Also, initiatives in this area feed into positive customer perceptions. The speeches that a CEO of NZ Food manufacturer makes on socially responsible business most definitely creates a positive perception of the company by consumers and thus is directly linked to increased sales from the supermarket shelf. As the *Jungle Book* song points out, "The hip bone is connected to the thigh bone."

The balanced scorecard in Exhibit 2.3 shows some of the likely CSFs that might be relevant in an organization.

Implications of the linking of performance measures to strategy "foundation stone" include:

- CSFs have to be determined in advance of the performance measures.
- Balanced scorecard methodology must be clearly understood.

Exhibit 2.3 Six-Perspective Balanced Scorecard

FINANCIAL Utilization of assets, optimization of working capital	**CUSTOMER** Increase customer satisfaction, targeting customers who generate the most profit	**ENVIRONMENT/ COMMUNITY** Supporting local businesses, linking with future employees, community leadership
INTERNAL Delivery in full on time, optimizing technology, effective relationships with key stakeholders	**EMPLOYEE SATISFACTION** Positive company culture, retention of key staff, increased recognition	**LEARNING AND GROWTH** Empowerment, increasing expertise, and adaptability

- The KPIs, performance indicators (PIs), and key result indicators (KRIs) that an organization is using should be linked. There should be an apparent common thread that is documented and reported to management via a report and to staff via a notice board and intranet page.

DEFINING VISION, MISSION, AND STRATEGY

Vision, mission, and strategy are often confused.

The *mission* is like a timeless "beacon" that may never be reached (e.g., a multinational in the entertainment business has a mission "to make people happy," and 3M's mission is "to solve unsolved problems innovatively").

The *vision* is where we want to go. The vision can galvanize your organization if it is stated with enough clarity, is time bound, and is supported continually by the senior management team (SMT). There are some very famous visions, most notably John F. Kennedy's when he said, "I believe that this nation should commit itself to achieving the goal, before this decade is out, of landing a man on the moon and returning him safely to the earth." This simple statement galvanized the U.S. scientific community, the management and staff of organizations involved in this endeavor in a herculean effort to achieve this vision. From the moment it was spoken, NASA experts began to plan how the millions of essential building blocks required to achieve this vision needed to be put together.

Strategy is the way an organization intends to achieve its vision. In a competitive environment, your strategy will distinguish you from your competition. In the public sector, your strategy determines the way you can best marshal your resources to achieve desired outcomes.

HOW TO IMPLEMENT WINNING
KPIs IN 16 WEEKS

Kaplan and Norton, in their groundbreaking book *The Balanced Scorecard: Translating Strategy into Action,* indicated that 16 weeks is sufficient time to establish a working balanced scorecard with KPIs. However, organizations of all sizes and complexity stumble with this process, and 16 weeks easily turns into 16 months. The key to success is to learn some key lessons:

- Find an external project facilitator.
- Begin with SMT commitment and education.
- Focus on the CSFs.
- Follow the 10/80/10 rule.
- Select a small KPI team.
- "Just do it."
- Use exiting systems for the first 12 months.
- Trap all performance measures in a database and make them available to all teams.

26

- KPI reporting formats are an art form, not a science.
- Maybe you need to rename.

Lesson 1: Appoint an External Project Facilitator

A suitably skilled external project facilitator is the key to success. Without this position being filled, dangers lurk everywhere. Throughout this manual you will see the important role the external project facilitator plays. The external project facilitator should be free of any proprietary applications, be well versed in performance measures, have well-rounded consultancy skills, have the credentials so that the SMT will listen and follow advice, and be able to motivate those he comes in contact with. His role will be full time for the first three weeks and then part time as the project team takes over. It is important that the external project facilitator's role takes a backseat, as a mentor would, as soon as possible as the project team gains confidence. Toward the end of the project there may be only a catch-up meeting once every two weeks, with key documentation being reviewed via e-mail in the intervening period.

Lesson 2: Begin with the Senior Management Team: Commitment and Education

The SMT attitude is crucial—any lack of understanding, commitment, and prioritizing of this important process will prevent success. It is common for the project team and the SMT to fit a KPI project around other competing, less important firefighting activities.

The SMT must be committed to the KPI project, to driving it down through the organization. Properly implemented, the KPI project will create a dynamic environment. Before it can do this, the SMT must be sold on the concept. This will lead to the KPI project's being treated as the top priority, which may mean the SMT's allowing some of those distracting fires to "burn themselves out."

There should be at least a half-day SMT workshop, where the external facilitator ensures that the entire executive team meets to understand the issues, the benefits, why current performance measures in use are never going to create the desired change and to workshop the critical success factors. After this workshop the SMT should be in a position to commit to it or put it back simmering on the company's "Aga" (a famous cooker).

The external project facilitator needs to ensure that the SMT understands its commitments. These commitments include setting aside time each week to perform exercises, including giving feedback on suggested measures, being available to the KPI team for interviews, visiting organizations that are successfully using KPIs, and constantly championing the KPI project in front of staff and management.

A senior consultant commented: Senior staff view the development of the BSC as an end in itself and go through the motions "to keep the boss happy." If the SMT is not strategic in its perspective and consequently does not see the BSC as a tool to help it better understand and manage the organization, this will be reflected in a loss of interest when the process of development gets tough, for example, when deciding on which KPIs to use and the trade-offs to be made. While the role of the SMT is important, the role of the CEO is critical. The CEO must be the central driver carrying the embryo BSC with him all the time, talking about it frequently, and so on.

Organizations sometimes find that support for the BSC flounders if a new CEO takes the helm before full implementation. It is important to sell, sell, sell the benefits to all new SMT members.

The BSC will help the organization rethink its strategies. Sometimes it may be better to redirect resources from the next strategic planning exercise into the KPI project.

Benefit of This Action. The SMT will get a buzz from being involved in a dynamic project, which will enhance understanding of their business and improve the implementation of their organization's strategies.

Lesson 3: Focus on the Critical Success Factors

Too often, time is spent debating the "perspectives," their names, and the design of the scorecard. The SMT loves this time of intellectualizing; however, it does not create much value. It is easy to get carried away with the debate, spending months ascertaining the perspectives while making little progress on defining the CSFs. *The CSFs determine the organizational health and vitality and where the organization needs to perform well.* KRIs, PIs, and KPIs are the actual performance measures, which naturally cascade from these CSFs. It is crucial that the SMT focus on providing the project team with CSFs. If this is done well, winning KPIs are much easier to find.

So what are the perspectives? Too much time can be spent debating whether there are four, five, or six perspectives and what their names are. Let me save you some trouble. You will need:

- One on the financials—call it *financial*
- One on (staff) learning and growth—call it *learning and growth*
- One on customer focus—call it *customer focus*
- One on internal business processes—call it *internal process*
- One on staff satisfaction—call it *staff satisfaction*
- One on environment/community—call it *environment/community*

To this end, the external facilitator needs to guide the SMT to accepting the perspectives recommended in this book.

Using the suggested six perspective names will mean that you are using a better practice perspective template for the first 6 to 12 months. After 12 months, the SMT and staff will be in a position of experience, knowledge, and understanding to fine-tune the perspective names to better suit the organization's needs.

Benefit of This Action   The SMT will invest the scarce time available to this project, scoring goals.

Lesson 4: Follow the 10/80/10 Rule

Kaplan and Norton recommend no more than 20 KPIs. Hope and Fraser[2] suggest fewer than 10 KPIs. The 10/80/10 rule is a good guide: 10 KRIs, up to 80 PIs, and 10 KPIs.

The external project facilitator's role is to ensure that the project team and SMT remain focused and concentrate on identifying those 10 KRIs, 80 PIs, and 10 KPIs that really matter. The external project facilitator needs to help the team differentiate between *key result indicators, performance indicators,* and *winning KPIs.*

Benefit of This Action   The KPI team will immediately focus on the end product (the 10/80/10), and not try to identify 80 KPIs in 200-odd performance measures.

Lesson 5: Select a Small KPI Team

KPIs can be designed successfully by a small team. Kaplan and Norton have seen BSCs designed successfully by an individual who had an in-depth understanding of the business.

Notwithstanding this possibility, a team approach with between two and four staff members is recommended. The external project facilitator, if involved right at the beginning, should help the SMT pick a team. Research into personnel records is recommended, as many talented staff are found in obscure places, some of which may have already had some KPI experience! The external project facilitator is looking for staff who have excellent presentation skills, knowledge of the organization and its market, a track record of innovation and completion, sound communication skills, and the ability to be cheerful under pressure (a recruiting trick of Sir Edmund Hillary). My suggestion is to find a blend of the oracles in the organization and team them up with "top guns"—young, fearless, and precocious leaders of the future who are not afraid to go where "angels fear to tread."

Exhibit 2.4   KPI Team Reporting Directly to the CEO

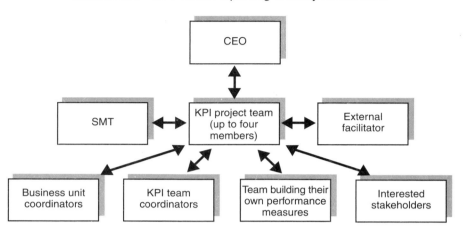

Once selected, this team must have a direct reporting line to the CEO (Exhibit 2.4). Any layer in between means that the SMT and CEO have not understood "SMT commitment."

The external project facilitator needs to convince management that these staff must be committed *full time* to the KPI project. Management will not complain if the project is completed ahead of schedule. The project team also needs to identify a liaison person (a coordinator) for each business unit and team. This person needs to be knowledgeable about their operation as their role is to be available to provide detailed knowledge about their area of operation to project team members, to provide feedback and to help run workshops.

The external project facilitator needs to convince members of the SMT not to include themselves in the project team. Including an SMT member in the team will lead to a string of canceled meetings as the senior manager is caught in the firefighting activities that is very much their reality. With the best willpower in the world, SMT members can never be fully focused on just one project.

Benefit of This Action   A carefully picked project team who, along with the coordinators, will have a good chance of success.

Lesson 6: "Just Do It"

The exact structure of result indicators, PIs, and KPIs is rarely right the first time. Kaplan and Norton agree with Nike and say "Just do it." The external project facilitator, SMT, and KPI project team need to ensure that the project culture is a "just do it" culture.

The external project facilitator's role is to ensure that the project team does not spend too much time on research. The key references are this KPI book and *The Balanced Scorecard: Translating Strategy into Action*.[3]

A "just do it" culture means that the team will not have to rely on external experts to run the project. CEOs are often wary of large projects that they perceive to be managed by expensive international consulting firms. The past decade is littered with six- or seven-figure consulting assignments, which have not delivered on the value expectations. A "just do it" culture brings the belief that the project team can do it. The external project facilitator's role here is to ensure that the project team remain confident (but not overconfident) and have picked up all the required skills they will need (e.g., delivering persuasive KPI presentations).

Benefit of This Action   The project will be protected against procrastination and have a good chance of implementing the KPIs within a 16-week period.

Lesson 7: Use Existing Systems for the First 12 Months

The project team should promote the use of existing in-house applications for the collection and reporting of the performance measures for at least the first 12 months. Much can be done with standard applications such as Excel, PowerPoint, SharePoint Team Services, and Access. There is often no need to purchase specialized software at this stage. Any such purchases can be done more efficiently and effectively 12 months down the track. The appropriate timing for implementing software to aid in the collection and deployment of KPI data will, however, vary from organization to organization. Some organizations may well have a resident application that performs this task well or may already know which application they will use for this task and thus can invest in the appropriate systems earlier.

The project team will be able to obtain better-practice performance measures and reporting formats from organizations specializing in better-practice reporting. Sophisticated intranet software is most likely available in-house, such as SharePoint Team Services, which is provided free of charge with FrontPage. These applications will help the team set up their intranet website so that anyone interested in the development of performance measures can obtain access. The team can provide preformatted lists with expiration dates to keep announcements current; and a place to collaborate on the development of KPI documentation and reports in real time.

The team will need to update the intranet site frequently themselves. It is too important to be left to a systems administrator who is not part of the project!

Benefit of This Action   Focusing on an immediate solution using existing in-house software will avoid the project time scale's being compromised by delays in prepurchase assessments, purchasing, and implementing a new system.

Lesson 8: Trap All Performance Measures in a Database and Make Them Available to All Teams

During the 16 weeks a number of performance measures will be found that, while not in the top ten KPIs, will still be highly relevant to business and service teams.

The project team needs to establish a database to record these measures and communicate them through a KPI intranet home page. It is suggested that the database include the following fields:

- Description of the performance measure
- Explanation as to how the performance measure is calculated
- The type of performance measure (KRI, PI, KPI)
- Person responsible for obtaining measurement
- System where data is sourced from or to be gathered
- Refinements that may be required to produce "real-time" information
- Which balanced scorecard perspective(s) the performance measure impacts
- Recommended display (type of graph, etc.)
- How often it should be measured
- Likely "cause-and-effect" relationship (e.g., if a late plane is brought back on time it will lead to . . .).
- Linkage of measure to the CSFs
- The required delegated authority that staff will need to have in order to take immediate remedial action
- The teams who have chosen to measure it (this can act like a selection list). You should have a column for each team with a "yes" or "✓" indicating selection.

The database should show not only what all the current teams' measures are but also any discarded measures. The project team can then help the teams, business units, and divisions with consistency and completeness (e.g., one measure devised by one team can and should be used by others, where appropriate).

During the 16 weeks, it is important that the project team purge the database on a regular basis to eliminate duplication and ensure consistency (e.g., the KPI team can suggest to one team "you may like to look at measure Y as teams A, B, and C are choosing to use it").

Benefit of This Action   This action will create a comprehensive and user-friendly resource for all.

Lesson 9: KPI Reporting Formats Are an "Art Form, Not a Science"

What is required is a reporting regime that thoroughly addresses those performance measures relevant to the CSFs and the six perspectives.

It is recommended that the SMT leave the design of the reporting formats (24/7, daily, weekly, and monthly reports) to the KPI team, trusting in their judgment. The SMT should tell the KPI project team that they will be happy to live with their sculpture knowing that they can always "keep the plinth and recycle the bronze 6 to 12 months down the track." It may require constant reminding by the external project facilitator to ensure this rule is followed by the SMT.

The key is to seek agreement that suggested modifications will be recorded and looked into at the end of the agreed review period. It will come as no surprise that many suggested modifications will not stand the test of time.

The KPI project team should make good use of the reporting templates provided in Chapter 5 before attempting to develop any of their own.

Benefit of This Action   This action leads to swift adoption of better-practice reporting templates.

Lesson 10: Maybe You Need to Rename

Key result indicators, PIs, and *winning KPIs* should ideally be structured within a balanced scorecard. However, across the world, there have been many failed BSCs principally due to "garbage in, garbage out."

The word *scorecard* may have negative connotations to management. What about *navigator, compass,* or other directional terms to help sell the concept and galvanize participation? Changing the name is particularly important where existing management have prior negative experiences with balanced scorecards.

Benefit of This Action   This action creates a KPI project name that helps galvanize the organization behind it.

Endnotes

1. Robert S. Kaplan and David P. Norton, *The Balanced Scorecard: Translating Strategy into Action.* Boston: Harvard Business School Press, 1996.
2. Jeremy Hope and Robin Fraser, *Beyond Budgeting: How Managers Can Break Free from the Annual Performance Trap.* Boston: Harvard Business School Press, 2003.
3. See note 1 above.

CHAPTER 3

Developing and Using KPIs: A 12-Step Model

This 12-step model (see Exhibit 3.1) is based on the four foundation stones (see Exhibit 3.2 and as outlined earlier in Chapter 2), the findings from organizations that participated in the original study,[1] and a ten-year journey of mine.

Many organizations that have operated with key performance indicators (KPIs) have found the KPIs made little or no difference to performance. In many cases, this was due to a fundamental misunderstanding of the issues. Organizations often begin to develop a KPI system by immediately trying to select KPIs without the preparation that is indicated in the twelve-step implementation plan. Like painting the outside of a house, 70% of a good job is in the preparation. Establishing a sound environment in which KPIs can operate and develop is crucial. Once the organization understands the process involved and appreciates the purpose of introducing KPIs, the building phase can begin.

Exhibit 3.1 12-Step Implementation Time Line

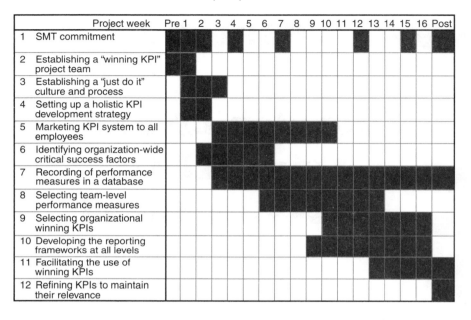

Exhibit 3.2 Four Foundations for KPI Development

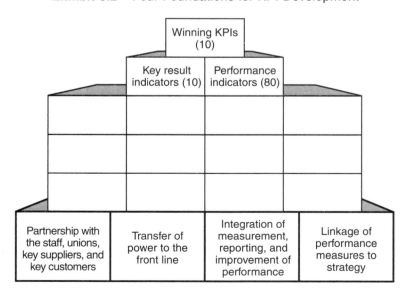

STEP 1: SENIOR MANAGEMENT TEAM COMMITMENT

Purpose

The SMT must be committed to developing and driving through the organization KPIs and any balanced scorecard (BSC) that includes them. SMT commitment creates a dynamic environment in which projects can thrive. Before the SMT can do this, they need to be "sold" on the concept and fully understand why they should treat monitoring and following up on the KPIs as a daily task.

SMT commitment requires the setting aside, on a weekly basis during the project, sufficient time to: give feedback on suggested measures during the weekly progress debrief; be available to the winning KPI team for interviews; visit other organizations that are using KPIs; and ensure that the team gets support to build the databases and reporting systems to trap and report measures. These systems should utilize available in-house software and act as a stop-gap until they are replaced, a year or so from the time the initiative started by more robust systems such as a specialist BSC application and a new executive information system, which will become the primary vehicles for recording and reporting KPIs.

The significance of CEO commitment, in particular, is emphasized in the following comment by a client: "I think senior staff can simply view development of KPIs as an end in itself and go through 'to keep the boss happy.' They are not strategic in their perspective so they don't see the KPIs and the associated BSC as tools to help them better understand and manage their organization. This can be reflected in a loss of interest when the process of development gets tough, such as deciding on KPIs to use and the trade-offs to be made. While SMT is important, I think the CEO is critical. The CEO must be the central driver and carry around the embryonic KPIs with them all the time, talk about it frequently, et cetera."

Another client pointed out that their BSC lost support when the CEO changed. It is thus important to continually sell the benefits to all *new* senior team members as soon as they come on the scene. In fact, prior positive experience with a BSC should be part of the person specifications. The last thing you need is an uninitiated CEO. They would be too high risk for the organization.

Key Steps for SMT Commitment

The KPI team will need to incorporate the following tasks among the work they perform in this step.

Task 1. *Appointment of a facilitator.* The CEO needs to locate an external facilitator, who will work with the SMT to scope the project, facilitate SMT commitment, help select the in-house KPI team, and support the KPI team in their journey of learning, discovery, and achievement. The facilitator needs to be experienced with performance measurement issues and given time to familiarize themselves with this book.

Task 2. *Facilitator delivers a half-day workshop to the SMT to kick-start the project.* This workshop (included in Chapter 4) will explain the new thinking on performance measures; convey the importance of monitoring and following up on the KPIs as a daily task; explain the difference between KRIs, PIs, and KPIs; and so forth. In the workshop the facilitator needs to ensure that the SMT understand the commitment required each week to giving feedback on suggested measures, being available to the project team for interviews, visiting other KPI sites, and so on. Before running the workshop the facilitator will send out the questionnaire in the KPI team resource kit.

Task 3. *Hold a one-day focus group meeting.* A cross section of staff, selected from 15 to 30 experienced staff covering the business units, teams, area offices, and head office, and covering the different roles from administrators to senior management team members, come to a central location to help the formation of a KPI project that will work. The morning session should be attended by the entire executive team. The session is run by an outside facilitator, who delivers presentations and facilitates the workshops (see draft program in Chapter 4). It is essential that all potential candidates for the KPI project team be present. As a result of this workshop, the project implementation program will be tailored to cover the main institutional barriers, and the SMT should be in a position to select the KPI team and commit to the project.

Task 4. ***Project team delivers two short workshops to the SMT during the project.*** These workshops (about two to three hours long) help maintain the interest of the SMT, gain valuable input, launch newly designed reports, and convey progress.

Task 5. ***Project needs to be sold to the SMT on emotional drivers, not logic.*** Remember, nothing was ever sold by logic! You sell through emotional drivers (e.g., remember your last car purchase). Thus, we need to radically alter the way we pitch this sale to the SMT and the board. We have to focus on the emotional drivers that matter to the SMT. Start by asking these questions:

- Does the lack of alignment of "daily activities" to strategy concern you?
- Are you overwhelmed by too many performance measures?
- Do you enjoy sifting through information overload in your precious family time?
- Are you missing goals through taking your eye off your critical success factors?

Then as part of the sale process point out to the SMT that:

- The previous performance measures have not changed anything.
- The focus on the right measures would mean the CEO and SMT would be more effective in less time, saving many long evenings/weekends of work.
- The right KPIs will link daily staff activities to the strategic objectives as they have never been linked before.
- This KPI project would start to transform the reporting into a decision-based tool with daily, weekly, and prompt monthly reporting that is interesting, concise, and prompt.
- The investment of time and money in the current performance measurement system is not generating enough value (estimate on the high side — costs motivate the SMT).

The project team needs to focus on the marketing of this new concept, budget holders will need to understand how this process is going to help them manage their business, and staff will need to understand that it is a positive experience enhancing their working life.

Many initiatives fail at this hurdle because we attempt to change the culture through selling logic, writing reports, and issuing commands via e-mail! It does not work. This project needs a public relations (PR) machine behind it. No presentation, e-mail, memo, or paper should go out unless it has been vetted by your PR expert. All your presentations should be road-tested in front of the PR expert. Your PR strategy should include selling to staff, budget holders, SMT, and the board.

If you were gifted at PR, you would most likely have chosen a different career! We have other gifts. If managed correctly, you would need only four to seven days of PR consultancy time. Avoid getting the PR expert caught up in lengthy meetings or writing original copy. Their role is to rework the output from the KPI team, working behind the scenes, often responding to e-mailed attachments once they have received an adequate debrief and have visited the organization.

The checklist in Exhibit 3.3 can be used as an aid to the KPI project team, ensuring that important tasks are not overlooked. The KPI team, with the facilitator, should amend this checklist before use to suit the organization and desired approach.

Exhibit 3.3   SMT Commitment Checklist
(FS = step that links to a foundation stone)

1. Is the CEO prepared to be the champion of this process?	❏ Yes ❏ No
2. If not, have you considered delaying the project until this level of commitment can be achieved?	❏ Yes ❏ No
3. Has all relevant background reading been provided for the SMT?	❏ Yes ❏ No
4. Has a presentation been made to the board and SMT to clarify the difference between KPIs, PIs, and KRIs? (FS)	❏ Yes ❏ No
5. Have you held a one-day focus group meeting?	❏ Yes ❏ No
6. Are the following SMT members willing to set aside time to be available for interviews and workshops?	
(Insert names)	❏ Yes ❏ No
	❏ Yes ❏ No
	❏ Yes ❏ No
	❏ Yes ❏ No
	❏ Yes ❏ No
	❏ Yes ❏ No
7. Are some of the SMT willing to set aside time for the occasional site visit to a better-practice organization?	❏ Yes ❏ No
8. Have likely candidates been selected for an in-house team to lead such a project?	❏ Yes ❏ No

(continues)

Exhibit 3.3 *(Continued)*

9. Have you persuaded the HR team to include prior positive BSC experience in the person specifications of all SMT positions?	❑ Yes ❑ No
10. Have you sold the project using adequate emotional drivers?	❑ Yes ❑ No
11. Have the SMT empowered the KPI team to make the decisions other than major investments? (FS)	❑ Yes ❑ No
12. Do the SMT fully understand the linkage between measurement, reporting, and performance improvement? (FS)	❑ Yes ❑ No
13. Do the SMT realize they will need to set aside time to make an important contribution in helping establish the critical success factors (CSFs) that link to the current strategies? (FS)	❑ Yes ❑ No
14. Has adequate marketing been performed on SMT members who are not fully supportive of the initiative?	❑ Yes ❑ No

Benefits of This Step The SMT appreciate being involved in a dynamic project, which enhances their understanding of their business, further develops their organization's business strategies, and links day-to-day activities to the strategic objectives.

STEP 2: ESTABLISHING A "WINNING KPI" PROJECT TEAM

Purpose

A small, well-trained team will have the best chance of success. Kaplan and Norton[2] have commented that KPIs have been successfully designed by an individual, without large consultations, but that this was an exception rather than the rule.

A project team of two to four people is recommended depending on the size of the organization. The chosen project team members need to be committed full time and report directly to the CEO. Any layer between the CEO and the team indicates that Step 1 has not been successfully achieved (see Exhibit 3.4). This point is so important that the project should not proceed if the CEO does wish to be involved in this way.

The KPI project team members should be a balanced mix of "oracles" and your "young guns." The latter are your young, fearless, and precocious leaders of the future, who are not afraid to go where angels fear to tread.

All business units and service teams should appoint a person to liaise with the KPI team who is sufficiently knowledgeable about their operation to provide information and feedback.

The interested stakeholders consist of those who can add a useful perspective to the project team, such as some members of the board, union representatives, representatives from some key suppliers, and key customers.

Do not include members of the SMT in the team, as they will be unable to meet the commitment required of being full time on this project.

Exhibit 3.4   Where the KPI Team Sits and Its Important Linkages

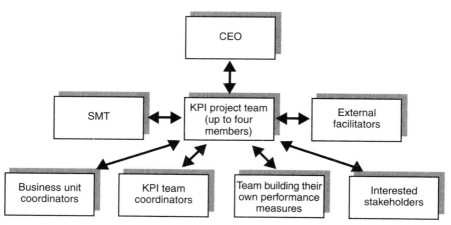

Key Tasks for Establishing a
Winning KPI Project Team

The KPI team will need to incorporate the following tasks among the work they perform in this step.

Task 1. ***External facilitator helps select the in-house KPI team.*** The external facilitator should help the SMT pick a team. Research into personnel records is recommended, as many talented staff are found in obscure places, some of which may have already had some KPI experience! The facilitator is looking for staff who have a proven track record of excellent presentation and communication skills, a flair for innovation, the ability to complete, knowledge of both the organization and sector, the aptitude to bring others on board, and the ability to be cheerful under pressure. The facilitator will use the questionnaire (see Chapter 4) in the selection process. It is advisable to run some tests to assess the potential compatibility of prospect team members, as it is likely they have never worked together on a large project before. The human resources (HR) manager will know about these tests.

Task 2. ***Facilitator negotiates for full-time commitment of KPI project team.*** The facilitator needs to convince management that these staff are required to be committed *full time.* Management will not complain if the project is completed ahead of schedule.

Task 3. ***Facilitator identifies coordinators.*** The facilitator also needs to identify a liaison person for each business unit or service team. This person needs to be knowledgeable about their operation, as their role is to provide the KPI team detailed knowledge about their area of operation to project team members, provide feedback, and so forth.

Task 4. *Facilitator develops training schedule and holds training exercises for the KPI project team.* For organizations over 3,000 staff the facilitator will be involved in training KPI teams in each main business unit. These teams will be support by a central team of trained in-house KPI consultants. The facilitator will train the in-house consultants who then will train the KPI teams as the rollout occurs.

The facilitator will need to establish the training gaps and set some team-building exercises for the team, which might include:

- Preparing a presentation to sell an idea
- Research exercises both through the company's files and the intranet, for example:
  - Find me the last five reports done internally on performance measurement issues.
  - Find me the articles and white papers written on the topic in major journals and respected websites.
- Going away for a weekend on a team-building excursion

The KPI team will need training and assistance. The type of training will include:

- A comprehensive understanding of this KPI book
- How to pass on knowledge using better-practice teaching techniques
- How to facilitate workshops, which they will be running
- How to deliver informative presentations
- How to design databases
- Better-practice communication techniques
- Maintaining a vibrant project team home page on the intranet (see exhibit in Chapter 4)

The checklist in Exhibit 3.5 can be used as an aid to the KPI project team, ensuring that important tasks are not overlooked. The KPI team, with the facilitator, should amend this checklist before use to suit the organization and desired approach.

Exhibit 3.5   Establishing a Winning KPI Team Checklist
(FS = step that links to a foundation stone)

1. Have a maximum of four staff been appointed to the KPI team?	❑ Yes	❑ No
2. Are at least half of the team working full time on the project?	❑ Yes	❑ No
3. Has the KPI team received all designated training? (It is important that all training needs noted in the planning phase have been addressed.)	❑ Yes	❑ No
4. Have all business units or service teams allocated a liaison person to work with the project team?	❑ Yes	❑ No
5. Have you been able to convince the SMT to step aside from project team responsibilities?	❑ Yes	❑ No
6. Are project team members a balanced mix of "oracles" and "young guns"?	❑ Yes	❑ No
7. Has the project team developed their intranet page to include:		
• Photos, CVs, interests, contact details of all team members?	❑ Yes	❑ No
• Linkage between performance measures (as they are being developed), and the organization's CSFs, strategies, vision, and mission? (FS)	❑ Yes	❑ No
• Database of performance measures as they are being developed?	❑ Yes	❑ No
• Useful reference material (articles, etc.)?	❑ Yes	❑ No
• Team scorecards as they are finished?	❑ Yes	❑ No
• Contact details of all the business unit coordinators?	❑ Yes	❑ No
• Implementation program and details about each step?	❑ Yes	❑ No
• A forum for sharing ideas, answering questions?	❑ Yes	❑ No
• Progress reports?	❑ Yes	❑ No

Exhibit 3.5   *(Continued)*

8. Have winning KPI team members been given an induction to this KPI book (understand the difference between KPIs, PIs, and KRIs, what critical success factors are, the foundation stones, the 12 steps, etc.)? (FS)	❏ Yes ❏ No
9. Have the winning KPI team been introduced to all the key stakeholders, ensuring that the key stakeholders fully understand and appreciate project requirements, the processes, and their role? (FS)	❏ Yes ❏ No
10. Has the delegated authority to the KPI team been finalized? (FS)	❏ Yes ❏ No
11. Have the team members previously demonstrated:	
• Excellent presentation skills?	❏ Yes ❏ No
• Innovation?	❏ Yes ❏ No
• Ability to complete large projects?	❏ Yes ❏ No
• Knowledge of the organization and sector?	❏ Yes ❏ No
• Advanced communication skills?	❏ Yes ❏ No
• Ability to bring others on board?	❏ Yes ❏ No

Benefits of This Step   The project will have a team that will have the capability to deliver, providing it is supported by a forward-thinking and supportive SMT. This team will have a good support network and have a vibrant and informative intranet home page.

STEP 3: ESTABLISHING A "JUST DO IT" CULTURE AND PROCESS

Purpose

"Right the first time" is a rare achievement, and creating winning KPIs is no exception. The resulting performance measure reports are just like a sculpture—you can be criticized on taste and content, but you can't be wrong. The SMT and "winning KPI" project team need to ensure that the project has a "just do it" culture, not one in which every step and measure is debated as part of an intellectual exercise.

The facilitator's role is to ensure that the project team does not spend too much time on research. In addition to this KPI book, the facilitator should ensure that the team is familiar with *The Balanced Scorecard: Translating Strategy into Action*[3] by Kaplan and Norton. There are many examples of reporting templates available on the World Wide Web that can be modified for use by your organization.

With this "just do it" culture and process comes a belief that we can do it—we do not have to rely on experts to run the project. In any case, many CEOs are extremely cautious of those large projects that they perceive to be primarily run by external consultants. It is worth noting that consultants, like artists, may not necessarily produce the sculpture that you want or need.

Establishing your winning KPIs is not complex, and the process should be carried out in-house, provided the team has the assistance of an experienced facilitator. The facilitator's role is principally that of a mentor to the project team and thus the facilitator should keep a low profile at the presentations.

There is no need to heavily invest in BSC applications during the first 12 months, as the team should be utilizing existing spreadsheet, presentation, and database applications. This eliminates the delay caused by having to tender, select, and populate specialized software at this stage. This can be done more efficiently and effectively in the second year of the project, when the organization has a better understanding of KPIs.

Applications such as SharePoint Team Services enable the KPI team to set up:

- Intranet pages that everyone with an interest in winning KPIs can access
- Preformatted lists containing memos and articles with expiration dates to keep announcements current

- Forums to discuss issues
- A place to collaborate on key winning KPI documentation and reports in real time
- A collaborative performance measure database

Key Tasks to Establish a "Just Do It" Culture and Process

The KPI team will need to incorporate the following tasks within the work they perform in this step.

Task 1. Provide training and support to teams so they can develop their performance measures. Major breakthroughs in performance improvement will result from the application of KPIs in local teams or work groups. This level of implementation is actually more significant than business unit–level or even organization-wide implementation. Recognize that significant educational resources and time are required to implement KPIs in teams.

Task 2. Introduce a moratorium on all existing KPIs. Every organization is likely to have a number of performance measures in place, even if they are not called KPIs. These existing measures need to be reviewed to fit them within the new three-tiered structure of performance measures (KRIs, PIs, KPIs). All new measures should only be allowed to be developed from the project, there being a moratorium on measures developed elsewhere.

The organizational emphasis on the existing KPIs will reduce as soon as SMT have been educated in what KPIs really are. All the existing measures will be included in the evaluation process with many being superseded.

Task 3. Check back to the foundation stones. When a consensus has been reached on the agreed process for developing and using

KPIs, a review must take place to ensure that all the steps are consistent with the four foundation stones of:

1. Partnership
2. Transfer of power to the front line
3. Integration of measurement, reporting, and performance improvement
4. Linkage of performance measures to strategy (to CSFs, BSC perspectives, and then back to the strategy)

Task 4. Validate process and plan with stakeholders. An agreed process and plan for introducing KPIs should be developed in consultation with management, local employee representatives, unions representing the organization's employees, employees, major customers, major suppliers, and the board. Many of the concerns held about introducing measurement can be overcome at this stage if the process for developing KPIs is validated by these stakeholders.

Task 5. Determining the perspectives of the balanced scorecard. Take a practical approach and avoid getting involved with debates on perspectives and their names. For the first year, stick to the names suggested below and focus your energies elsewhere:

You will need a name for each of these perspectives:	Why not call the perspective:
Financial performance	Financial
Development of staff	Learning and growth
Customer satisfaction	Customer focus
Internal processes, innovation, use of new technology, etc.	Internal process
Staff satisfaction	Staff satisfaction
Relationship with the environment and the community	Environment/community

Staff satisfaction and environment/community are both important considerations and should not be omitted from your BSC. The latter is also important because it means the winning KPI will incorporate all triple-bottom-line issues (environment, social, and financial) as well as retaining the consistency with Kaplan and Norton's work).

The checklist in Exhibit 3.6 can be used as an aid to the KPI project team, ensuring that important tasks are not overlooked. The

Exhibit 3.6   Establishing a "Just Do It" Culture and Process Checklist (FS = step that links to a foundation stone)

1. Has the process largely been driven by in-house resources?	❑ Yes ❑ No
2. Have you ensured that the process will help cultural consistency?	❑ Yes ❑ No
3. Have you reviewed all the implementation steps and confirmed that they build on the foundation stones?	❑ Yes ❑ No
4. Has the SMT openly supported and promoted a "just do it" culture?	❑ Yes ❑ No
5. Has the project intranet page emphasized the "just do it" culture?	❑ Yes ❑ No
6. Have you introduced a moratorium on existing KPIs?	❑ Yes ❑ No
7. For the first 12 months, are existing spreadsheet, reporting, and database applications being utilized?	❑ Yes ❑ No
8. Have the SMT ensured that the stakeholders have been consulted and have contributed to the thinking on:	
• The initial purpose of the introduction of KPIs?	❑ Yes ❑ No
• The uses and application of KPIs?	❑ Yes ❑ No
• The initial spread and penetration of KPIs throughout the entire organization?	❑ Yes ❑ No
• The pace at which KPI introduction and implementation will proceed?	❑ Yes ❑ No
• The training and education required to empower employees to create their own KPIs? (FS)	❑ Yes ❑ No

(continues)

Exhibit 3.6 *(Continued)*

9. Has the SMT announced that it has delegated authority to the KPI team and will abide by their decisions? (FS)	❑ Yes ❑ No
10. Have the appointed coordinators in business units and teams been given an induction to the processes (understand the difference between KPIs, PIs, and KRIs, what are critical success factors, the foundation stones, the 12 steps, etc.) (FS)	❑ Yes ❑ No
11. Has the project team accessed a KPI database?	❑ Yes ❑ No

KPI team, with the facilitator, should amend this checklist before use to suit the organization and desired approach.

Benefits of this Step   Establishing a "just do it" culture and process will enable the project team to cut through red tape and deliver a timely suite of performance measures, recognizing that it will require further tailoring and improvement at a review period, six to eight months down the road.

STEP 4: SETTING UP A HOLISTIC KPI DEVELOPMENT STRATEGY

Purpose

This step involves placing the KPI project in a total holistic strategy for achieving "best practice." It is important to map an overall strategy for organizational change, noting the purpose and role of KPIs within this entire process. In addition, it is necessary to consider how best to run the implementation.

The most appropriate implementation is influenced by the size of the organization, the diversity of the business units, the organization's locations, and the in-house staff resources available for the project. Each implementation is like a finger print, unique to the organization, and should be designed in consultation with the stakeholders, the external facilitator, and prior experiences on what has worked and not worked in past implementation rollouts.

There are a number of questions to answer. Is this the right time to embark on this process? Do we have a window of the time to commitment to this project? How should we best implement winning KPIs across our organization? Have we maximized the fit with the other changes our organization is pursuing to achieve world-class performance? When you can answer these questions clearly, you will be able to locate KPIs in the total performance improvement game plan.

Key Tasks for Setting Up a Holistic KPI Development Strategy

The KPI team will need to incorporate the following tasks within the work they perform in this step.

Task 1. Ascertain the existing measurement culture. Be aware of the current understanding of performance measurement and how it has been used in the organization. It takes time to adapt new approaches to performance measurement. It is therefore important to plan the introduction to KPIs with an appreciation of the organization's existing comfort (or discomfort) levels with performance measurement. The rollout will need to take into account the location of subsidiaries, the current significance of their operation, and their long-term future (e.g., there may be no point embarking on a rollout to a foreign subsidiary if it is to be sold).

Task 2. KPI project phased approach. For organizations with less than 500 staff, a total rollout in 16 weeks is achievable. Organizations with over 500 full-time employees (FTEs) will require a phased approach. The larger the organization, the more focused the first phase must be. For a 100,000-FTE multinational, the first phase would be limited to one of the core businesses, where the benefits are the greatest, and include the head office units, as these must be able to support this process early on. See Exhibit 3.7, which shows the indicative rollout duration for different sizes of organizations.

For organizations with more than 3,000 employees, there will be KPI teams in each main business unit. These teams will be supported by a central KPI team. This central KPI team, who will be trained by the facilitator, will effectively be a team of in-house KPI consultants who travel in pairs to support the KPI teams in each main business unit. The size of the central KPI team varies according to the speed of roll out required.

The number of in-house consultants can be supplemented by external consultants provided they have been trained in the methodology.

Exhibit 3.7   Indicative Rollout Duration (use as guide only)

Size of organization (FTEs)	500	500–3,000	3,000–10,000	10,000+
First phase (two-person KPI project team)	18 weeks (small organizations will need at least 10 weeks)	16–20 weeks for first phase	Too small	Too small
First phase (four-person KPI project team)	16 weeks (small organizations will need at least 10 weeks)	16–20 weeks for first phase	20–26 weeks for first phase	20–30 weeks for first phase
Rollout phases	Not required	10 weeks for each rollout phase	10 weeks for each rollout phase	10 weeks for each rollout phase

The required number of trained in-house KPI consultants will vary depending on the complexity of the rollout and prior experience from other project rollouts in the organization.

Each rollout can be performed by trained business unit project teams, who will be supported by a designated KPI project team member. It is unlikely that more than three business units can be rolled out simultaneously because there will be inadequate support from the central KPI team.

Subsequent rollout in other countries and business units will meet different types of resistance and hurdles. Business units in Asia may require a higher number of workshops than those in Europe or vice versa.

Task 3. ***Once started, ensure that every roll-out phase is completed within a 16-week time frame.*** The rollout success will be dependent on maintaining a momentum and energy. Once a business unit or subsidiary has been selected, there should be an intensive push to complete. Each rollout phase should not be allowed to take more than 16 weeks, as the groundwork has been prepared. A rollout in a business unit could be as little as a 10-week period. It is unlikely to be shorter due to the level of consultation and the team performance measures workshop rollout.

Task 4. ***Be flexible about the rate of progress required.*** KPIs do not have to be applied uniformly within the organization. Typically, the drive to introduce KPIs originates from senior or corporate levels of management, but it can also be pushed up from within the organization. Where flexibility is allowed, different parts of the organization can proceed with the introduction of KPIs at varying paces, according to their own requirements and readiness.

A flexible approach to the development of KPIs avoids at least two potential problems associated with centralized, universal implementation:

1. Too much top-down influence on KPI selection, resulting in a lack of ownership in the measures and resistance to their use

2. Difficulties associated with coordinating and resourcing KPI development in several business units, departments, and work groups at the same time.

Three examples of the approach taken when introducing KPIs are presented in Exhibits 3.8, 3.9, and 3.10. In each case, it is possible to observe how KPIs were integrated or aligned with change and improvement strategies.

The checklist in Exhibit 3.11 can be used as an aid to the KPI project team, ensuring that important tasks are not overlooked. The KPI team, with the facilitator, should amend this checklist before use to suit the organization and desired approach.

Exhibit 3.8 Approach 1: Manufacturing Site of an Individual Business Division

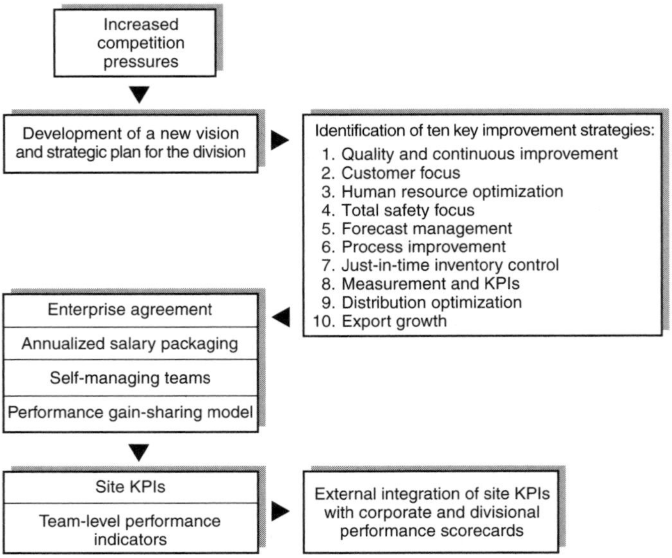

Increased competition pressures

↓

Development of a new vision and strategic plan for the division ▶ Identification of ten key improvement strategies:
1. Quality and continuous improvement
2. Customer focus
3. Human resource optimization
4. Total safety focus
5. Forecast management
6. Process improvement
7. Just-in-time inventory control
8. Measurement and KPIs
9. Distribution optimization
10. Export growth

Enterprise agreement
Annualized salary packaging
Self-managing teams
Performance gain-sharing model ◀

↓

Site KPIs
Team-level performance indicators ▶ External integration of site KPIs with corporate and divisional performance scorecards

Exhibit 3.9   Approach 2: Total Organization

Strategic review of
direction and
operations of total
organization

▼

Focus on developing

Continuous improvement culture   ▶ ▶ ▶ ▶ ▲

Business and service orientation

▼   ▼

New business management model:
- Leadership
- Strategic planning
- Management by fact
- People management
- Customer focus
- Continuous improvement
- Business results

Performance reporting project:
To improve the quality of
performance reporting
throughout the organization
and to the board

▲ ▼
▲ ▼
▲ ▼

▼

Six critical success factors for the
organization

Performance-reporting workshops   ▶ ▶ ▶ ▶ ▼ ◀

Key performance indicators in
divisions, departments, and
business units

Exhibit 3.10   Approach 3: Large Manufacturing Site
Encompassing Six Business Units

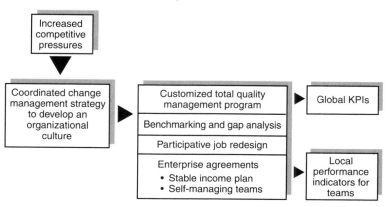

Increased
competitive
pressures

▼

Coordinated change
management strategy
to develop an
organizational
culture

▶

Customized total quality
management program   ▶ Global KPIs

Benchmarking and gap analysis

Participative job redesign

Enterprise agreements
- Stable income plan
- Self-managing teams

▶ Local
performance
indicators for
teams

The focus for the change strategy: Embrace total quality management (TQM) and
benchmarking

Purpose of introducing KPIs: To facilitate benchmarking and as an outcome of job
redesign

Exhibit 3.11   Setting Up a Holistic KPI Development Strategy
Checklist (FS = step that links to a foundation stone)

1. Are you prepared to explain why KPIs are necessary?	❑ Yes ❑ No
2. Are you prepared to allow KPIs to develop and evolve?	❑ Yes ❑ No
3. Have the stakeholders reached agreement on the initial purpose, spread, and penetration of KPIs throughout the entire organization? (FS)	❑ Yes ❑ No
4. Have the stakeholders reached agreement on the pace at which KPI introduction and implementation will proceed? (FS)	❑ Yes ❑ No
5. Have you evaluated the existing measurement culture in your organization?	❑ Yes ❑ No
6. Have you defined what "world-class performance" is in your organization?	❑ Yes ❑ No
7. Have you defined the changes that your organization is introducing to achieve "world-class performance"?	❑ Yes ❑ No
8. Has an internal PR campaign been established to help remove the suspicions that might exist among staff? (FS)	❑ Yes ❑ No
9. Have the SMT agreed to the provision of training and education required to empower employees to create their own performance measures and take immediate remedial action when necessary? (FS)	❑ Yes ❑ No
10. Have the SMT provided a coherent integrated framework of strategies and critical success factors that linked to the BSC perspectives?	❑ Yes ❑ No
11. Has a decision been made as to whether KPIs are going to be developed for the whole organization or just specified business units?	❑ Yes ❑ No
12. Can you be flexible about the rate of progress required?	❑ Yes ❑ No

Benefits of This Step   A coherent approach will be established that should encourage employee, SMT, board, and union buy-in and commitment.

STEP 5: MARKETING THE KPI SYSTEM TO ALL EMPLOYEES

Purpose

Employees must be prepared for change. The project team and the SMT need to:

- Convince employees of the need for change with open and honest information sharing.
- Spell out what change is required.
- Show how KPIs contribute to the broader change strategy.
- Attract employees' interest so that they want to participate.
- Address employee resistance to change and performance measurement.

A formal briefing program should be held to outline the changes associated with introducing KPIs into the organization. By its conclusion all employees should at least believe that they need to do something differently, and a core group should be clear about implementation issues and how performance measures will be used. Those who have shown an aptitude for the new KPI model should become the team coordinators, who will support and help the KPI team to develop and implement KPIs.

Key Tasks for Marketing KPIs to All Employees

The KPI team will need to incorporate the following tasks within the work they perform in this step.

Task 1. ***Run a survey on a cross section of staff.*** A survey is required to find out the current perceptions on existing performance information in the organization, the current concerns about the new project, and what needs to be covered in the employee briefings. With the help of the HR team, make a selection of experienced staff covering all regions, levels of staff, and so forth. This cross-section sample should not be greater than 200 or 10% of total staff and not less than 50 staff. With these numbers you can close of the survey with a 60% return rate and still have a valid survey. Too large a sample will make data mining more difficult and seldom raise any new issues. The questionnaire is set out in the resource kit.

*Task 2. **Build a case for change with PR support.*** Demonstrate that KPIs are part of an SMT agreed package of initiatives to respond to the pressures on the organization. Spell out these pressures in terms that people can understand. Use comparative information from preliminary benchmarking to highlight the performance gap between your organization and best practice. It is important to utilize the services of an expert in public relations.

Remember, nothing was ever sold by logic! You sell through emotional drivers. Thus, we need to radically alter the way we pitch this sale to the staff. We have to focus on the emotional drivers that matter to them:

- The right mix of performance measures will make work more rewarding and enjoyable, e.g., greater staff recognition.

- The focus on the right measures would mean their work would be more effective, e.g., their day-to-day work would be better linked to the organization's strategic objectives.

- Over time, they would have more empowerment and autonomy, e.g., staff making more decisions.

- Winning KPIs will enhance profitability and thus offer greater job security and possibly increased remuneration, e.g., through profit-sharing arrangements.

Many initiatives fail at this hurdle because we attempt to change the culture through selling by logic, writing reports, and issuing commands via e-mail! It does not work. This project needs a PR machine behind it. No presentation, e-mail, memo, or paper should go out to staff unless it has been vetted by your PR expert. All your presentations should be road-tested in front of the PR expert.

Task 3. *Use the vision to attract the staff.* Generate interest in KPIs by painting a picture of how the workplace could look in two to three years once KPIs and other initiatives have taken hold. Over time, empowered staff will begin to generate their own versions of the vision for the workplace. However, in the beginning, it is critical that the KPI project team be passionate about the task. The PR expert is to ensure that all documentation sells this vision adequately, e.g., in memos, presentations, and the KPI team intranet pages.

Task 4. *Roll out a road show to all staff.* Structure road-show briefings so that all employees hear the message, taking into account language skills, literacy, and shift-work patterns. It is important to demonstrate the existence of a partnership in change by ensuring that employee/union representatives also address staff attending the road show covering the purpose for introducing KPIs.

The best workshops seem to be held in informal workplace settings, involving local management known to the audience, which are managed to maximize feedback, e.g., in larger groups the use of question slips will aid this process. A suggested road-show program is presented in Chapter 4.

Address the issues and perceptions raised in the employee survey that are important to your audience through small group briefings, spelling out the workplace vision. The briefings are used to explain the purpose and use of KPIs, address any concerns, spell out ground rules and the way forward.

Employees are often concerned that performance information will be:

- Collected on individuals and held against them, e.g., for disciplinary purposes
- Controlled by management
- Filtered both in content and distribution (e.g., "They only show us information when it suits their purposes")
- Used to allocate blame for performance problems

Task 5. Illustrate "Where to next?"—the intranet KPI home page.
Introduce the staff to the project team intranet KPI home page and show them how to use it. Describe the steps required to develop and implement KPIs, indicate key employee roles, and publish a time frame for process completion. A time frame shows you are committed. Having published one, demonstrate the necessary discipline to achieve it.

The checklist in Exhibit 3.12 can be used as an aid to the KPI project team, ensuring that important tasks are not overlooked. The KPI team, with the facilitator, should amend this checklist before use to suit the organization and desired approach.

Exhibit 3.12 Marketing the KPI System to All Employees Checklist (FS = step that links to a foundation stone)

1. Have you delivered joint briefings to employees with SMT, project team, and union representatives presenting on the same platform? (FS)	❑ Yes	❑ No
2. Has all material been reviewed by a PR expert? (FS)	❑ Yes	❑ No
3. Have initial briefings specifically addressed employee concerns by stressing the consultative, training-related processes by which employees in teams will develop their own KPIs.	❑ Yes	❑ No

Exhibit 3.12 *(Continued)*

4. Has a broad vision of what change is required been spelled out?	❑ Yes ❑ No
5. Have you sold the need for KPIs through emotional drivers that mean something to the employees?	❑ Yes ❑ No
6. Have you described the next steps in the process of developing and implementing winning KPIs?	❑ Yes ❑ No
7. Have you indicated the key roles for employees to play?	❑ Yes ❑ No
8. Has the SMT set aside funding for in-house workshops to be rolled out covering all teams?	❑ Yes ❑ No
9. Have the project team and the SMT addressed people's concerns about change and performance measurement?	❑ Yes ❑ No
10. Has sufficient interest been aroused so employees want to participate in the KPI project?	❑ Yes ❑ No
11. Have you used success stories to help sell the message?	❑ Yes ❑ No
12. Have you provided training on how employees can best use the KPI project home page?	❑ Yes ❑ No
13. Have you published a time frame with appropriate milestones and a realistic deadline?	❑ Yes ❑ No

Benefits of This Step   Marketing the KPI system to all employees maximizes the commitment from a broad cross section of employees.

STEP 6: IDENTIFYING ORGANIZATION-WIDE CRITICAL SUCCESS FACTORS

Purpose

The relationship between CSFs (also referred to as key result areas) and KPIs is vital, as illustrated in Exhibit 3.13.

CSFs identify the issues that determine organizational health and vitality. When you first investigate CSFs, you may come up with 30

Exhibit 3.13   Journey from a Mission and Vision
to Performance Measures that Work

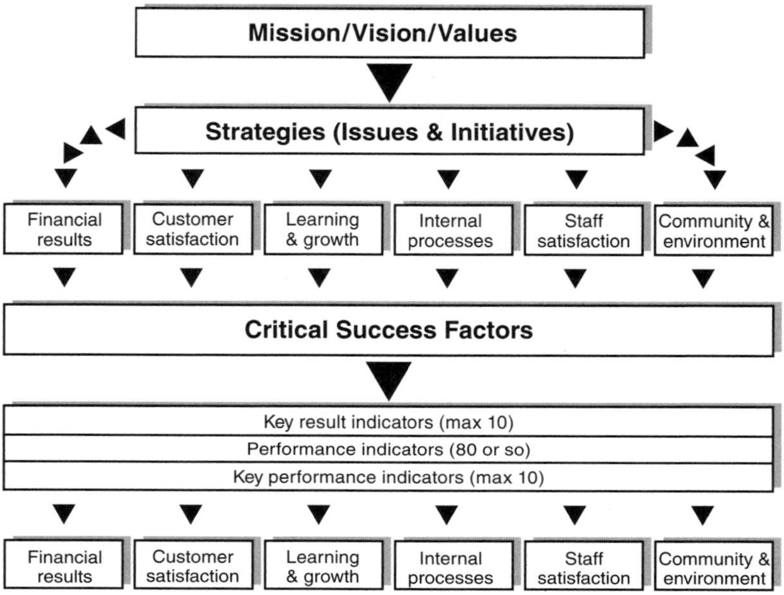

Mission/Vision/Values

▼

Strategies (Issues & Initiatives)

Financial results	Customer satisfaction	Learning & growth	Internal processes	Staff satisfaction	Community & environment

Critical Success Factors

▼

Key result indicators (max 10)
Performance indicators (80 or so)
Key performance indicators (max 10)

Financial results	Customer satisfaction	Learning & growth	Internal processes	Staff satisfaction	Community & environment

or so issues that can be argued are critical for the continued health of the organization. The second phase of thinning them down is easy, as the more important CSFs have a broader influence cutting across a number of BSC perspectives (e.g., the timely arrival and departure of planes impacts nearly all the BSC perspectives of an airline; see the following example).

Example

"Timely arrival and departure of planes" impacted all six BSC perspectives. Late planes:

- Increased cost in many ways, including additional airport surcharges and the cost of accommodating passengers overnight as a result of late planes being "curfewed" due to noise restrictions late at night (financial perspective)

Example   *(Continued)*

- Meant unhappy customers and alienated those people affected by the late arrival of the passengers, possible future customers (customer satisfaction perspective)

- Created a negative impact in the wider community and thus reduced the potential pool of future employees (community perspective)

- Caused waste of food — hot food has a short serving window and waste of fuel as planes endeavored to make up for lost time and operated outside their most economical flight speed (environmental perspective)

- Had a negative impact on staff development, as staff would repeat the bad habits that had created late planes (learning and growth perspective)

- Adversely affected supplier relationships and servicing schedules, resulting in poor service quality (internal process perspective)

- Led to employee dissatisfaction, as they had to deal both with frustrated customers and the extra stress each late plane created (employee satisfaction perspective)

Better practice suggests that organizational CSFs should be limited to between *five and eight* regardless of the organization's size. However for a conglomerate, the CSFs will largely be industry specific, e.g., the CSFs for an airline are different from the CSFs for a retail record chain store. Thus a collection of CSFs for a conglomerate would be greater than the suggested five to eight. The selection of the CSF is a very subjective exercise and the effectiveness and usefulness of those CSFs chosen is highly dependent on the degree of analytical skill of those involved. Active leadership by senior management in this step is thus mandatory.

Too often, time is spent debating the balanced scorecard perspectives, their names, and the design of the scorecard with little progress on determining what the CSFs are.

Key Tasks for Identifying Organization-Wide Critical Success Factors

The KPI team will need to incorporate the following tasks within the work they perform in this task.

Task 1. ***Consult strategic planning documents.*** Review all the strategic documents in your organization, then draw and develop CSFs from these. Review the SMT meeting notes, the output from the SMT workshop, the output from the focus group workshop, and the SMT survey conducted in Step 1, "Senior Management Team." Complete the worksheet in Chapter 4. Check that your proposed CSFs address all six of the following performance perspectives:

1. Customer focus
2. Financial performance
3. Learning and growth
4. Internal process
5. Employee satisfaction
6. Environment and community

You will find that some CSFs cover more than one perspective (e.g., the timely arrival and departure of planes impacts nearly all the perspectives). This is a sign that it is a core CSF.

Task 2. ***Project team to develop a robust way to build a hierarchy of critical success factors.*** Good techniques to locate the five to eight critical success factors include:

- CSF relationship mapping
- Using weightings in a workshop setting
- Strategy mapping if you have the software
- Cross-checking the CSFs against how many of the six BSC perspectives they impact

All these methods are set out in Chapter 4.

An example of how CSF relationship mapping can be used on the whiteboard with the draft CSFs is shown in Exhibit 3.14.

An example of how cross-checking the CSFs against how many of the six BSC perspectives they impact is shown in Exhibit 3.15.

There has been much discussion about documenting "cause-and-effect" relationships, and the relationship mapping process is a derivative of this and a quicker process. In

Exhibit 3.14   CSF Relationship Mapping

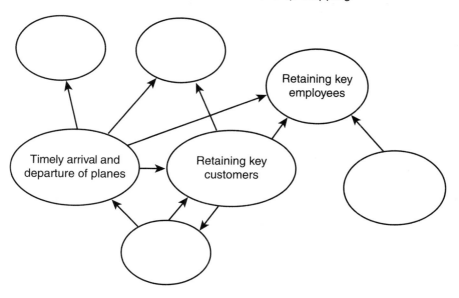

Exhibit 3.15   Checking Impact of CSFs against the Six BSC Perspectives

Critical Success Factor	Financial	Customer Satisfaction	Staff Satisfaction	Learning and Growth	Internal Process	Environment/ Community
1. For example, timely arrival and departure of planes	✓	✓	✓	✓	✓	Possible
2. For example, delivery in full and on time	✓	✓	Possible	✓	✓	
3. Etc.		✓			✓	✓
4. Etc.	✓					

workshops attendees find they can do a first cut of this exercise in under an hour. If project teams use a cause-and-effect relationship process, they need to be careful not to get sidetracked by it. It can become an interesting intellectual process going nowhere.

The aim of cause-and-effect relationships is to understand and document likely human behavior (e.g., if a late plane is brought back on time it will lead to . . . . The likely actions of staff will be to . . .).

Task 3. **Hold a workshop to revisit your CSFs.** Invite members of the focus group, along with others who have shown an aptitude in this area, to a one-day workshop. There are break-out sessions where workgroups of up to six people will brainstorm this issue. Use the workshop format in Chapter 4.

Task 4. **Finalize CSFs after consultation with stakeholders and employees.** Once draft CSFs have been prepared, review with the SMT, the board of directors, identified stakeholders (relevant CSFs with key customers and key suppliers), an employee focus group, and with the employee union representatives.

Task 5. ***Explain the CSFs to employees.*** Once final CSFs have been agreed on, communicate them to all management and staff.

The checklist in Exhibit 3.16 can be used as an aid to the KPI project team, ensuring that important tasks are not overlooked. The KPI team, with the facilitator, should amend this checklist before use to suit the organization and desired approach.

Exhibit 3.16   Identifying Organization-Wide CSF Checklist
(FS = step that links to a foundation stone)

1. Have you reviewed all the strategic documents?		
• Vision statement	❑ Yes	❑ No
• Mission statement	❑ Yes	❑ No
• Values statement	❑ Yes	❑ No
• Strategic plan	❑ Yes	❑ No
2. Have you covered the following in your search for your organization's performance CSFs?		
• An analysis of economic, social, political, environmental, and technological trends that will shape the general context in which the organization operates (sometimes referred to as an environmental scan)	❑ Yes	❑ No
• Analysis of the markets in which the organization operates and identification of future trends and developments	❑ Yes	❑ No
• Review of current expectations and satisfaction levels of the organization's *key* customers	❑ Yes	❑ No
• Analysis of likely *future* customer expectations and requirements	❑ Yes	❑ No
• Review of current supplier performance and likely future requirements and the status of those relationships or partnerships	❑ Yes	❑ No
• Analysis of the financial status of the organization and the available capacity to meet future requirements	❑ Yes	❑ No
• Review of the human resource capabilities of the organization, taking into account the future requirements identified	❑ Yes	❑ No

(continues)

Exhibit 3.16 *(Continued)*

2. Search for CSFs *(continued)*	
• Review of the existing organizational culture and its appropriateness for meeting the anticipated challenges	❏ Yes ❏ No
3. Have you short-listed five to eight CSFs?	❏ Yes ❏ No
4. Has a robust process been followed to ensure that the CSFs will stand the test of time?	❏ Yes ❏ No
5. Do the CSFs address all six of the perspectives?	❏ Yes ❏ No
6. Have you consulted with employee representatives? (FS)	❏ Yes ❏ No
7. Have you consulted key customers?	❏ Yes ❏ No
8. Have you consulted with key suppliers?	❏ Yes ❏ No
9. Have you consulted with representatives of the board?	❏ Yes ❏ No
10. Have you advised all employees what CSFs are and how they were selected?	❏ Yes ❏ No
11. Have you tested the short-listed CSFs to ensure that they link back to the organization's strategy?	❏ Yes ❏ No

Benefits of This Step Employees and management understand what CSFs are and can therefore focus their attention on finding performance measures in these areas, that is, performance measures that will make a real difference.

STEP 7: RECORDING PERFORMANCE MEASURES IN A DATABASE

Purpose

The KPI team will have gathered and recorded performance measures from information gained during discussions held with senior management, revisiting company archives, reviewing monthly reports, and external research from the beginning of the project. There will also be many performance measures generated from each team workshop.

Performance measures identified need to be collated in a database. This database needs to be up-to-date, complete, and made available to all employees to help support their understanding of performance measures and to assist with their selection of their team measures.

The database should include the following fields:

- Description of the performance measure

- Explanation as to how the performance measure is calculated

- The type of performance measure (KRI, PI, KPI)

- Person responsible for obtaining measurement

- System where data is sourced from or to be gathered

- Refinements that may be required to produce "real-time" information

- Which balanced scorecard perspective(s) the performance measure impacts

- Recommended display (type of graph, etc.)

- How often it should be measured

- Linkage of measure to the CSFs

- The required delegated authority that staff will need to have in order to take immediate remedial action

- The teams who have chosen to measure it (this can act like a selection list). You may have a column for each team with a "yes" or "✓" indicating selection.

These fields could be set out as shown in Exhibit 3.17.

Exhibit 3.17   Performance Measures Database Layout Example

Name of performance measure	Calculation of measure	Type of PM (KRI, PI, KPI)	Person responsible	System where data is going to be gathered	BSC perspective	Recommended display (e.g., type of graph)	Frequency of measurement (24/7, daily, weekly, monthly)	Linkage to critical success factors	Team xx	Team xx	Team xx	Team xx	Team xx	Team xx	Suggested target	Required reliability/accuracy (±5%, ±10%, ±20%)	Estimated time to gather information (15 mins, 30 mins, 1 hour, 1/2 day, 1 day, > 1 day)
Number of initiatives implemented from the quarterly rolling client survey	Number of initiatives implemented out of total arising from survey	PI	JAK	Word	CF	Number	Weekly	1 Retain key customers 2 Increased repeat business	✓	✓	✓				All by 3 months post survey	± 5%	5 mins

Key Tasks for Recording Performance Measures in a Database

The KPI team will need to incorporate the following tasks within the work they perform in this step.

Task 1. *Select a database that has wide access and is user friendly.* Most organizations operate database applications, which are underutilized. The KPI team must learn to use the in-house database application and design and build a performance measure database that is easy to use.

Task 2. *Populate the database.* On a daily basis the measures that have been identified need to be input into the database to ensure that they are not lost in a mountain of paperwork. In order to maintain consistency of input, a person or small team should be responsible for this action. An easy-to-use input form should be set up in the database to facilitate entering the measures in a timely manner.

Task 3. *Train all teams to use the database and to constantly refine the performance measures.* The KPI team needs to train all the other teams on not only how to use the database, but also the significance of each database field. This is best achieved through the rolling workshops they will be giving teams. Teams will be trained to review the database to see if any new measure has emerged that is very relevant for their team. This will be performed as part of a later step.

The team will need to constantly refine the performance measures by "peeling more layers off the onion." In time, a clearer hierarchy of measures will develop, some will be discarded, and new measures will start emerging that will have a profound impact on the organization's future.

Task 4. *Ensure that all database fields are complete for every performance measure.* The project team needs to constantly review the database, cleanse it of duplication, and encourage teams to look at measures that have been selected by their peers.

The checklist in Exhibit 3.18 can be used as an aid to the KPI project team, ensuring that important tasks are not overlooked. The KPI team, with the facilitator, should amend this checklist before use to suit the organization and desired approach.

Exhibit 3.18 Comprehensive Recording of Measures in Database Checklist (FS = step that links to a foundation stone)

1. Have you spoken to the information systems team to identify databases for which your organization holds current licenses?	❏ Yes ❏ No
2. Have you sourced an in-house expert to help you set up the database?	❏ Yes ❏ No
3. Have all KPI team members been up-skilled so they can update daily the new database?	❏ Yes ❏ No
4. Does each team and business unit coordinator have access to the performance measure database? (FS)	❏ Yes ❏ No
5. Is the database being reviewed on a weekly basis to ensure consistency of input? (KPI project team members and team coordinators will be entering data)	❏ Yes ❏ No
6. Are all the database fields being used appropriately?	❏ Yes ❏ No
7. Is the database recording the delegated authority staff need to take immediate corrective action on issues affecting each identified KPI? (FS)	❏ Yes ❏ No
8. Is there a selection column for all teams so they can extract the measures that appear appropriate?	❏ Yes ❏ No
9. Are all teams using the database to select their measures?	❏ Yes ❏ No
10. Is the database available to all staff (perhaps on a read-only basis)? (FS)	❏ Yes ❏ No

Exhibit 3.18   *(Continued)*

11. Have you piloted the database training workshop material to ensure that it informs and educates?	❑ Yes ❑ No
12. Have you checked to ensure that the database has been updated for every workshop held?	❑ Yes ❑ No

Benefits of This Step   Recording measures in a database checklist creates a vital electronic working tool for the KPI project team and for teams selecting and recording their performance measures. This tool will ensure a high level of consistency throughout the organization.

STEP 8: SELECTING TEAM-LEVEL PERFORMANCE MEASURES

Purpose

This is a vital step in performance improvement. The appropriate team performance measures will help teams to align their behavior in a coherent way to the benefit of the entire organization. This is achieved because teams are focusing on those performance measures that are linked to the organization's CSFs.

Team performance measures will be comprised mainly of PIs and some of the organization's KPIs, where relevant (e.g., a late planes measure would have been monitored by the front desk, engineering, catering, cleaning, etc. but not the accounting team).

While management often tends to become focused on achieving KPI introduction at the global, organization-wide level, in reality the critical issue is getting these KPIs embedded in the teams that need to take corrective action 24/7.

Thus, it is at the team level—level 4 in Exhibit 3.19—that significant and sustainable performance improvement can be achieved through the use of performance measures.

77

Exhibit 3.19 Interrelated Levels of Performance
Measures in an Organization

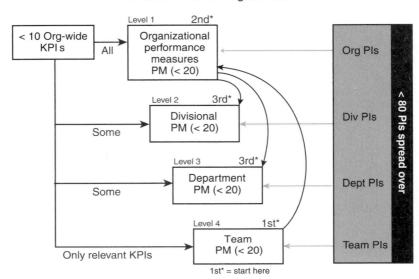

Why Team Performance Measures Are Critical

Every CEO would wish that the employees' day-to-day work aligns itself with the organization's strategic objectives. Yet this is seldom the case. Why does the marketing team measure all customer satisfaction infrequently when our CSF in that area might be "increased repeat business from key customers"? Surely we should be measuring the satisfaction of our key customers regularly and ignoring those customers who we could do without. Why is that dispatch does the same quality control and timely dispatch procedures for all customers when it is our key customers that should get extra checks at the expense of those customers who we would be better off losing? The answer lies with the fact we have not communicated the critical success factors to staff, nor have we worked with them to select the measures that stem from these CSFs. Once we have performed this, a magical alignment can occur between effort and effectiveness.

There are two types of teams in most organizations:

1. **Self-managing or self-directed work team.** This type of team contains a group of employees that have a broad, cross functional membership, which effectively allows members to confront most of the issues that affect production or service delivery. Self-managing teams typically set their own objectives, develop their own procedures, and share the roles traditionally performed by supervisors and middle management. Self-directed teams operate at a higher developmental level, often exercising autonomous responsibility over major planning and scheduling issues.

2. **"Managed" work groups or teams.** These teams are those in the traditional model that have a supervisor/manager who is the focus for direction and leadership and the provider of performance feedback.

In both cases, the team is the level at which performance measures should be developed.

Key Tasks for Selecting Team-Level Performance Measures

The KPI team will need to incorporate the following tasks within the work they perform in this step.

Task 1. Have teams complete pre-workshop worksheets. The worksheets in Chapter 4 should be completed by all teams involved in this process.

Task 2. Roll out training workshops to all teams. Training and assistance must be provided by the KPI project team to all teams so that they are equipped to select their own performance measures that are consistent with the organization's CSFs. It is a good idea to bring a number of teams together at the same time, as they will learn from each other's different views. Some workshop groups have up to 80 attendees doing the team performance measures exercise. Each team is broken into a discussion group of four to seven staff members. The workshop program is set out in Chapter 4.

Encourage a balance in team performance measures. If the CSFs are clearly defined and related to the six BSC perspectives (customer focus, financial performance, learning and growth, internal process, employee satisfaction, and environment/community), then team performance measures developed in this context will generally reflect the required balance.

Use the mind-mapping techniques set out in Chapter 4 during the brainstorming sessions (see Exhibit 3.20 for an example).

Task 3. ***Promote an appropriate mix of past, current, and forward-looking measures.*** The previous debate about lag (outcome) and lead (performance driver) indicators is now dispensed with. The term *lead indicator* was always difficult to understand because it applied to both past and future measures (see Exhibit 3.21).

Key result indicators replaces the term *outcome measures,* and PIs and KPIs are now categorized as either past, current, or future measures. Current measures are those measured 24/7 or daily. You will find that most of the KPIs in your organization will fit into the *current or future categories,* as nearly all KPIs will be measured 24/7, daily, or at least weekly (e.g., late planes were measured 24/7; see Exhibit 3.22).

Task 4. ***Permit team performance measures to evolve.*** Virtually no team will achieve a perfect set of performance measures at its first or even its second attempt. Further, once a set of performance measures exists, individual indicators may need

Exhibit 3.20   Mind-Map Worksheet Example

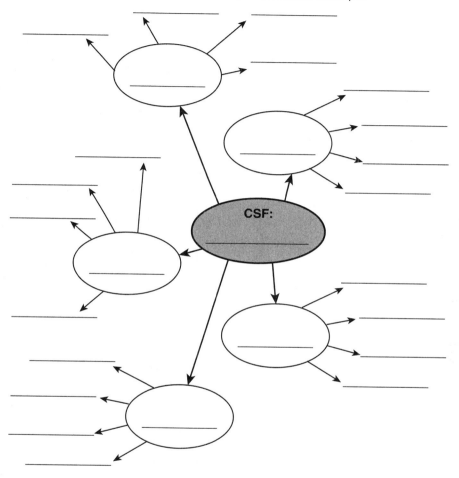

to vary as the team improves performance and then moves on to focus on other problem areas.

Task 5. *Use Pareto's 80/20 rule when assessing how to calculate a measure.* Encourage teams to be practical when assessing how to calculate their chosen performance measures. It is essential that the cost of gathering the measure is not greater

Exhibit 3.21 Replacing the *Lead/Lag* Terms

Lead/Lag Way	KRI/PI/KPI Way with Past, Current, and Forward-Looking Measures
Customer acquisition/retention rate (lag indicator)	*KRI* Customer acquisition/retention rate
Policyholder satisfaction survey	*PIs* **Past:** Customer satisfaction of the top 10% of policyholders **Current:** Top 10% of policyholders who have made a complaint/sought a credit note/activated a guarantee today **Future:** Number of *planned* visits to the top 10% of policyholders next week/two weeks/month (weekly measure)

than the benefit derived from the measure. For many measures, staff should be encouraged to either use sample techniques, e.g., measure late invoices one week a month or assessment techniques, e.g., estimate the number of coaching hours received last month. Pareto's 80/20 rule encourages us to only measure in detail the KPIs—the performance measures (e.g., the late planes tracking system would have warranted a multimillion-dollar investment).

Task 6. Never lose sight of team ownership. Remember that the primary purpose of team performance measures is to assist

Exhibit 3.22 Taking a Past Measure and Looking at It as a Current and Future Measure Example

Past Measures	Current (24/7 and Daily) Measures	Future Measures
Number of late planes this month	Late planes in the air over two hours late	Number of initiatives to be implemented this month to target areas that are causing late planes

and help the team to improve their performance. It follows that their performance measures represent what they want to collect in order to contribute to improvement in the identified CSFs. The KPI team needs to gently steer them if they are off course.

Task 7. A maximum of 25 performance measures for a team. As a guide, 25 performance measures is probably the upper limit that a team should select for regular use. Any more than this number may lead to resource problems and a lack of focus. These performance measures will include some of the organization's KPIs. Some teams may have two organizational KPIs, while others have up to five of the organization's KPIs in their team scorecard. Some head-office teams will not have KPIs in their scorecard, as they are not relevant to them.

Remember that the KPIs affect the entire organization. Thus, there are no KPIs specific to one team. These measures are PIs, not KPIs.

The checklist in Exhibit 3.23 can be used as an aid to the KPI project team, ensuring that important tasks are not overlooked. The KPI team, with the facilitator, should amend this checklist before use to suit the organization and desired approach.

Exhibit 3.23 Developing Team Performance Measures Checklist (FS = step that links to a foundation stone)

1. Have you fully analyzed performance measures detailed in this book and those from KPI workshops? (See www.waymark.co.nz.)	❑ Yes ❑ No
2. Do all team members clearly understand the characteristics of KPIs?	❑ Yes ❑ No
3. Have teams been given sufficient time (during standard work hours) to explore their performance measures in a stimulating environment?	❑ Yes ❑ No
4. Are the CSFs clearly defined? (If not, delay until they are.)	❑ Yes ❑ No

(continues)

Exhibit 3.23 *(Continued)*

5. Have teams tied performance measures to organizational CSFs and processes rather than the confines of their sphere of influence?	❏ Yes ❏ No
6. Are teams being practical about performance measurement? (Precision is required only with critical performance measures)	❏ Yes ❏ No
7. Are the PIs owned by the teams?	❏ Yes ❏ No
8. Have the employees been trained and encouraged to accept the delegated empowerment to fix issues when a KPI is off track? (FS)	❏ Yes ❏ No
9. Have teams checked back to ensure that they have covered all the CSFs with performance measures? (FS)	❏ Yes ❏ No
10. Have teams restricted PI numbers to a maximum of 25 measures?	❏ Yes ❏ No
11. Have teams populated the database with their agreed performance measures? (This will help other teams and ensure greater consistency.)	❏ Yes ❏ No

Benefits of This Step   Selecting team-level performance measures puts measures in place that:

- Clarify the teams' objectives.

- Align daily team work to the organization's strategic objectives.

- Improve job satisfaction, e.g., measures that increase the level of staff recognition.

- Increase job security as teams contribute more to the bottom line.

- Provide a basis for recognizing and celebrating team achievements.

- Provide a better understanding and link to the organization's strategies.

STEP 9: SELECTING ORGANIZATIONAL "WINNING KPIs"

Purpose

It is recommended that the selection of organizational KPIs be started after progress has been made at the team level (level 4 in Figure 3.19). The KPI team will have gained an insight into the organizational KPIs by working with teams. It is very much an iterative process, with findings being conveyed both up and down. Once levels 1 and 4 (in Exhibit 3.19) are in a semifinalized state, the back-filling of the divisional or departmental measures (levels 2 and 3) can take place. This process will ensure a cascading relationship of measures.

This approach reflects the goal of empowerment and will ensure team ownership of their performance measures. It will also ensure that as performance measures are introduced at other levels in the organization, they will be influenced by:

- The organizational CSFs

- The vital activities existing at the workplace that are creating success or failure

No matter how complex your organization—whether a public body, a hospital, or a diverse manufacturer—*team, department, and division performance measures should not be consolidated* to become the organization measures. This ends up in chaos, e.g., some hospitals have over 200 measures at the organizational level.

It is crucial that all staff members fully understand KPIs (see Chapter 2). Remember, finding appropriate KPIs is very much like peeling the layers off an onion to get to the core. While it is relatively easy to produce a reasonable list of performance indicators, it is difficult to identify the *key* performance indicators, particularly when it is remembered that there will be fewer than ten in the entire organization.

Key Tasks for Selecting Organizational "Winning KPIs"

The KPI team will need to incorporate the following tasks within the work they perform in this step.

Task 1. Ensure that KPIs and PIs are balanced. The organization's KPIs and PIs should address all six BSC perspectives (customer focus, financial performance, learning and growth, internal process, employee satisfaction, and environment/community). The worksheet in Chapter 4 will assist with this process.

Task 2. Limit the organization-wide KPIs to no more than ten. There is no magic number, but few organizations will need more then ten KPIs, and, in fact, many can operate successfully on fewer than five KPIs.

Task 3. Permit the KPIs and PIs to evolve. Virtually no KPI project team will achieve a perfect set of KPIs and PIs at its first or even its second attempt. Further, once a set of KPIs exists, information from the teams will shed light on enhancements to the KPIs.

Task 4. Ensure that all KPIs have most or all of the KPI characteristics. Ensure that all KPIs selected pass this checklist. See Chapter 4 for the layout for the form. The characteristics of a KPI are:

- Nonfinancial measures (not expressed in dollars, yen, euros, etc.)
- Measured frequently (e.g., daily or 24/7)
- Acted on by CEO and senior management team
- Understanding by all staff the measure and what corrective action is required
- Responsibility tied to the individual or team

- Significant impact (e.g., it impacts most of the core CSFs and more than one BSC perspective)
- Has a positive impact (e.g., affects all other performance measures in a positive way)

The checklist in Exhibit 3.24 can be used as an aid to the KPI project team, ensuring that important tasks are not overlooked. The KPI team, with the facilitator, should amend this checklist before use to suit the organization and desired approach.

Benefits of This Step   Organizational winning KPIs are measures that will have a profound impact on the organization, stimulating

Exhibit 3.24   Selecting Organizational Winning KPIs Checklist (FS = step that links to a foundation stone)

1. Do the organization-wide KPIs and PIs cover all BSC perspectives?	❏ Yes ❏ No
2. Are the organization-wide KPIs and PIs consistent with the current strategies?	❏ Yes ❏ No
3. Have the organization-wide KPIs and PIs been discussed with the relevant key stakeholders? (FS)	❏ Yes ❏ No
4. Have KPIs selected been limited to ten or less?	❏ Yes ❏ No
5. Are the SMT and particularly the CEO still committed to champion the organizational KPIs and PIs?	❏ Yes ❏ No
6. Have all KPIs been included in all team performance measures where it is relevant?	❏ Yes ❏ No
7. Do KPIs make sense to the teams?	❏ Yes ❏ No
8. Have you put every KPI through the KPI checklist?	❏ Yes ❏ No
9. Has the SMT given formal delegated authority to the relevant employees to fix issues affecting any KPI? (FS)	❏ Yes ❏ No
10. Have you checked that KPIs do not include KRIs or PIs?	❏ Yes ❏ No
11. Have plans been put in place to build systems to report KPI movement as it occurs?	❏ Yes ❏ No

timely action and linking day-to-day activities to the strategic objectives of the organization.

STEP 10: DEVELOPING THE REPORTING FRAMEWORK AT ALL LEVELS

Purpose

The reporting framework must accommodate the requirements of different levels in the organization and the reporting frequency that supports timely decision making. A suggested framework for reporting performance measures is set out in Exhibit 3.25.

Most KPIs should be reported each day (electronically) at 9 A.M. or, as in the case of late planes, constantly updated 24 hours a day, 7 days a week.

In most organizations there will be another "top five" KPIs that will need to be reported at least weekly (excluding the daily KPIs already identified). One weekly measure that is important in most organizations is the reporting of late projects and late reports to the SMT. Such reports will revolutionize completion in your organization.

The remaining PIs can be reported monthly along with team, department, divisional, and organization-wide BSC reporting.

The board should receive only a one-page governance "dashboard" on the KRIs. These KRIs cover the well-being of the organization and

Exhibit 3.25   Suggested Reporting Framework

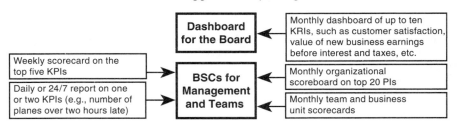

are not PIs or KPIs. They should cover the six BSC perspectives, and to do this may require tracking up to ten KRIs. In any one month, only those KRIs that are telling the more important stories must be reported. It is desirable not to give the board the management BSCs because their role is one of governance, and giving them management information diverts them from their true role.

The reporting stage is open to procrastination, and thus it is important to ensure that the "just do it" attitude is operational. It is not uncommon to find teams spending considerable time debating which colors are the most appropriate in presentations to senior management. It is important that this is not allowed to occur on the KPI project.

It is recommended that the SMT leave the design of the BSC template to the KPI team, trusting in their judgment. The SMT should tell the KPI project team that they will be happy to live with their sculpture knowing that they can always "keep the plinth and recycle the bronze" 6 to 12 months down the road. What you are looking for is a reporting framework that covers the measures in the six BSC perspectives. The key is to seek agreement that suggested modifications will be recorded and looked into at the end of the agreed review period. It will come as no surprise that many suggested modifications will not stand the test of time.

The reporting template examples shown in Chapter 5 are provided to stimulate ideas. These formats could serve as useful templates for the first six months of operation, leaving management and the KPI team to concentrate on the measures. Most measures should have their own trend graph and the intranet is the ideal tool to hold these graphs. In addition, each team should have a performance notice board that is covered with trend graphs of their monthly measures.

The daily and weekly measures will be driven by systems and recorded and reported on the intranet and be available to all relevant staff. KPIs will affect many teams across the organization, and thus all KPIs should be available, via the intranet, to all staff. The more exposure that can be given to KPIs, the better the resultant ownership, understanding, and performance outcomes.

Getting Action to Happen in the Right Direction

If the CEO, members of the SMT, and management focus on the KPIs every day, staff will naturally follow suit. The CEO spending 30 minutes a day asking for explanations from managers and staff about a wayward KPI will soon create focus. It certainly will be seen that receiving two phone calls from the CEO is not a good career move! In other words, the CEO should "walk the talk" and always know where the KPIs are heading at any point during a day. Thus, on out-of-office trips, the CEO should be able to link into the intranet and obtain an update of the KPIs.

The system will have failed if the review process relies on structured, regular meetings at each level where KPIs are in operation. Remember, KPIs are indicators that need monitoring, reporting, and action 24/7!

Staff may require training to help them understand the actions they can and need to take to correct wayward KPIs. Empowerment must take place to ensure staff have the resources and freedom to take action.

Key Tasks for Developing the Reporting Frameworks at All Levels

The KPI team will need to incorporate the following tasks within the work they perform in this step.

Task 1. Provide appropriate training on reporting. The project team should train the teams on how best to report their measures using a combination of the intranet, notice boards, and hard copy. They should also give training on how to complete these reports efficiently. KPI reporting should be almost instantaneous—once appropriate systems are in place, weekly and monthly reporting should also be quick routines. A team BSC should, as a guide, be no more than half a day's preparation and be delivered to the team by the close of the first working day of the new month. Late reporting has no place in performance measurement.

Staff will need much help with maintaining a Pareto 80/ 20 view. There is no point spending a lot of time playing around with spreadsheets as the information will be too late to be of any use.

Use the report formats in Chapter 5.

Task 2. Establish a suite of meaningful graphs that are easy to understand. While there is a vast array of graphical techniques for displaying KPI data, it is recommended that you follow the following rules:

- *Big and bold*—each graph should be at least a quarter of an A4 page to promote ease of reading and attract attention.

- *Consistent*—It is recommended that graph standards are maintained for at least six months before updating.

- *Trend analysis*—to show movement over at least the last 15 to 18 months if you have a seasonal business. Remember, business has no respect or interest in your year-end; it is merely an arbitrary point in time.

- *Range*—to show the acceptable range, which may be cascading over time, to indicate expected improvements.

- *Keep graphs simple*—Each graph should be clear even to an untrained eye (e.g., while waterfall, radar, amd three-dimensional graphs might look nice, they can be misunderstood by staff and thus are rarely necessary).

The exact use of recommended graph techniques is discussed in Chapter 4.

- *Quick to update* — all graphs should be in a system that enables swift updating, and in some cases they should be automated to enable 24/7 analysis via the intranet. Graphs should not slow down the monthly management BSCs and the board dashboard reporting process, which should be completed by no later than day three post month end.

- *Accessible* — graphs should be accessible to all staff via the intranet.

- *Do not show a budget line* — there is no room to show a flawed monthly or year-to-date budget line, an arbitrary apportionment of the annual planning number that was done at the last minute and was wrong from the very start. It is like setting your race plan for the America's Cup regardless of the wind conditions on the day of racing.[4]

- *Key turning points* — insert notes on the graphs explaining major turning points.

- *Insert a title that is meaningful to the reader* — e.g., title like "return on capital employed (ROCE) is moving up well" instead of just saying "ROCE."

- *Use a colorful layout* — this will help comprehension, and it is a good idea to use a light yellow–colored background with four to five light gray–colored gridlines.

See suggested graph layouts in Chapter 5.

Task 3. Develop a hierarchy of reports to staff, management, and the board. If KPI reporting is not available 24/7 and is not the focus of action and discussed at performance improvement meetings, attention will wane and the graphs will become a symbol of frustration, rather than the focus for continuous improvement.

The checklist in Exhibit 3.26 can be used as an aid to the KPI project team, ensuring that important tasks are not overlooked. The KPI team, with the facilitator, should amend this checklist before use to suit the organization and desired approach.

Exhibit 3.26 Developing Display, Reporting, and Review Frameworks at All Levels Checklist (FS = step that links to a foundation stone)

1. Has the KPI team been given the delegated authority to finalize the reporting framework?	❑ Yes ❑ No
2. Have you based reporting around a decision-based process? (e.g., avoiding the trap of large, late information memorandums that do not help the decision-making process)	❑ Yes ❑ No
3. Have you accessed some better-practice reporting templates?	❑ Yes ❑ No
4. Have you developed separate reporting for the board (based around key result indicators)?	❑ Yes ❑ No
5. Have you developed a team BSC template that teams can complete easily using existing company systems?	❑ Yes ❑ No
6. Have you developed an organizational scorecard for the SMT?	❑ Yes ❑ No
7. Have you developed an organizational scorecard for staff?	❑ Yes ❑ No
8. Have you developed 24/7 and daily reporting of KPIs on the intranet?	❑ Yes ❑ No
9. Have you developed weekly reporting of KPIs on the intranet?	❑ Yes ❑ No
10. Is there a moratorium on changing reports and graphs for at least six months?	❑ Yes ❑ No
11. Have you established company graph standards that comply with better practice?	❑ Yes ❑ No

(continues)

Exhibit 3.26   *(Continued)*

12. Have you marketed and supplied electronic templates of these graphical standards to all teams?	❏ Yes ❏ No
13. Are there notice boards where staff can see these measures in "hard copy"?	❏ Yes ❏ No
14. Can the relevant stakeholders access the KPIs that are relevant to them? (E.g., the union should be advised if "delivery in full, on time" is becoming an issue.) (FS)	❏ Yes ❏ No

Benefits of This Step   A consistent reporting regime will be developed based around decision-based reporting techniques, which will not absorb too much of management's time.

The reports will encourage empowered staff to undertake corrective action immediately on issues that are adversely affecting KPIs (e.g., in an airline, staff being empowered to immediately increase the cleaning contractor's staff to ensure a quicker turnaround of a late plane).

STEP 11: FACILITATING THE USE OF WINNING KPIS

Purpose

Many organizations have performed good KPI work only to have it fail or become buried when key staff move. It is thus important that the use of KPIs becomes widespread in an organization and is incorporated into its culture.

The SMT's role is crucial. It is important that they lead by example by using the KPIs at their disposal and seeking explanation immediately when any of the KPIs are trending in the wrong direction. Ideally, you are looking for an environment where management and staff expect a phone call from the SMT if a KPI was turning in the wrong direction. The staff and management will thus do everything in their power to avoid that situation.

In turn, the SMT must be committed to empowering staff to take immediate action (e.g., it is reported that Toyota empowered staff on the shop floor to stop the production line if they find any defect in a car they are working on which cannot be fixed while the line is going).

Resources must be allocated so that continual education and communication can be maintained. This should not be the responsibility of just the KPI project team.

Key Tasks for Facilitating Use of KPIs

The KPI team will need to incorporate the following tasks within the work they perform in this step.

Task 1. *Constantly reassure the SMT so that they are confident to empower the frontline staff.* It is essential that the SMT learn to relax their control and empower their staff. Without staff empowerment, the effectiveness of KPIs is limited, as staff respond to management direction rather than learning to become proactive themselves.

Task 2. *Roll out a video road show for all staff.* The video includes an introduction from the CEO and a presentation on "the new thinking on key performance indicators" by a skilled presenter from the project team. It is essential to explain to staff how the chosen KPIs are to operate, who is to collect data and by when, the systems to be used, the monitoring and action to be taken by SMT, and the delegated empowerment that employees have to correct situations as the rise on a 24/7 basis. This video is then followed by a workshop which is set out in Chapter 4.

Task 3. Avoid setting performance measures too far into the future.
If you set a target in the future, you will never know if it was
appropriate given the conditions of that period (e.g., if the
target was too hard or too soft).

***Task 4. Have relative performance measures that are compared
against other organizations.*** Jeremy Hope and Robin Fraser,
pioneers of the Beyond Budgeting methodology,[5] have
pointed out how KPIs can easily end up in the trap of an
annual fixed performance contract. In other words, if you
set a target in the future, you will never know if it was appropriate given the particular conditions of that time. You often
end up paying incentives to management when in fact you
have lost market share. In other words, your rising sales did
not keep up with the growth rate in the marketplace.

Relative performance measures are an important addition to KPIs; for example, you may focus on all planes in
the air that are flying more than two hours late 24/7, but,
in addition, compare total late flights, average turnaround
times, number of missing passengers, and so forth, to other
airlines. This could perhaps be carried out quarterly using
a benchmarking company.

Another benefit of relative measures is that they do not
need alteration (e.g., if being in the top quartile or 2% above
the norm is the relative measure, then this benchmark does
not need changing).

***Task 5. Ensure that there are a mix of past, current, and future per-
formance measures.*** Most measures across the world are past
measures and in a bid to rectify this the terms *lead indicators* and *lag indicators* were introduced. As mentioned in
Chapter 2, these terms do not work for KPIs, e.g., the "late
plane" KPI could be called a lag indicator because it reports

past events, but while the plane is still in the air and running late it is still about to create chaos for passengers, suppliers, and airline staff at the destination airport and therefore is also a lead indicator.

Task 6. Set KPIs as ranges, not a single target. Establishing an acceptable range is more beneficial than a fixed target, as a range takes into account the vagaries of the future and so is more tolerant of environmental change (e.g., a set of goal-posts rather than a single thin post at the end of the playing field).

It is a good idea to show the "acceptable range" cascading up or down over time to indicate expected improvements; see Exhibit 3.27.

Exhibit 3.27   Ranging KPIs

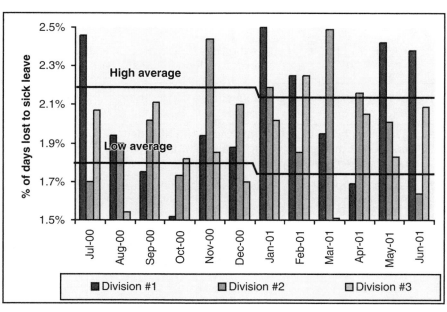

Task 7. Apply the 10/80/10 rule. Ensure that the final performance measures in use comply with the 10/80/10 rule as follows:

- Up to ten key result indicators should be maintained, with only five to eight to be shown to the board at any one time.

- Eighty performance indicators are sufficient for most organizations, especially when standard measures are used across all teams (e.g., a training-days measure should be applied consistently with the same definition and graphical illustration across all teams).

- For many organizations, ten KPIs will be more than adequate. Some may wish to extend to up to 20, but be careful—the more KPIs you use, the less focus you have.

The checklist in Exhibit 3.28 can be used as an aid to the KPI project team, ensuring that important tasks are not overlooked. The KPI team, with the facilitator, should amend this checklist before use to suit the organization and desired approach.

Exhibit 3.28 Facilitating the Use of KPIs Checklist
(FS = step that links to a foundation stone)

1. Have current strategies been adequately conveyed to the teams?	❏ Yes ❏ No
2. Have all staff who are to operate with a KPI attended a workshop covering what the KPIs are, how they operate, what delegated authority staff have, etc.?	❏ Yes ❏ No
3. Has the KPI rollout been undertaken in conjunction with all the stakeholders?	❏ Yes ❏ No
• Management	❏ Yes ❏ No
• Employee representatives	❏ Yes ❏ No
• Key customers	❏ Yes ❏ No
• Key suppliers	❏ Yes ❏ No
• Unions	❏ Yes ❏ No
4. Are the SMT actively supporting the empowerment of staff? (FS)	❏ Yes ❏ No

Exhibit 3.28 *(Continued)*

5. Are the senior management team monitoring the KPIs on a daily basis and following up shortfalls with relevant staff?	❑ Yes	❑ No
6. Have outdated performance measures been removed?	❑ Yes	❑ No
7. Have KPIs been set up with relative comparisons where relevant (e.g., comparisons to third parties)?	❑ Yes	❑ No
8. Have some KPIs been established as a range rather than a target?	❑ Yes	❑ No
9. Have you ensured that performance measures are a mix of past, current, and future measures?	❑ Yes	❑ No
10. Have you avoided the use of the terms *lead* and *lag* *indicators*?	❑ Yes	❑ No
11. Is the KPI still together, albeit maybe on a part-time basis?	❑ Yes	❑ No
12. Are you providing one-to-one training, where necessary, to ensure that staff commit time to taking accurate measurements of performance, understand the reports, and are motivated to take action in the appropriate time frames?	❑ Yes	❑ No
13. Is the KPI team giving ongoing help to teams who are using KPIs and PIs?	❑ Yes	❑ No
14. Is there a mixture of KRIs, PIs, and KPIs following the 10/80/10 rule?	❑ Yes	❑ No
15. Are the SMT and particularly the CEO focusing on the KPIs every day?	❑ Yes	❑ No
16. Are the SMT actively championing staff who have correctly used their delegated authority to rectify a situation? (FS)	❑ Yes	❑ No

Benefits of This Step   The performance measures in your organization (the KPIs, PIs, and KRIs) are being applied properly and are given the opportunity to create the desired change.

STEP 12: REFINING KPIs TO MAINTAIN THEIR RELEVANCE

Purpose

It is essential that the use and effectiveness of KPIs be maintained. Teams will modify and change some of their KPIs and PIs as priorities change during their journey of process improvement. It is simply a case of moving on to the next priority area for improvement, as the previous ones have been mastered and behavior alignment has been locked in. However, some KPIs should always be maintained because of their relevance to the organization-wide CSFs; for example, for an airline, the late plane KPI will always be used. In addition, it is likely that KPIs relating to customer focus and workplace culture will always remain in place.

Teams will also need to amend and build new measures to respond to the emergence of new CSFs. The new CSF will be identified during quarterly rolling planning phases.

Work groups should review and modify their own KPIs and PIs on a periodic basis, certainly not more frequently than every six months.

Key Tasks for Refining KPIs to Maintain Their Relevance

The KPI team will need to incorporate the following tasks within the work they perform in this step.

Task 1. Review organization-wide CSFs at least annually. The environment in which we operate is changing so rapidly that the requirements for survival and then prosperity can change markedly within a year. CSFs must be reviewed on a continuing planning cycle. As a better practice, it can be part of the quarterly rolling planning regimen. As part of this process, you will need to complete the worksheet in Chapter 4.

Task 2. *Hold a one-day focus group revisiting the performance measures.* The objectives of the workshop are to revisit the performance measures with a key group of staff and management and to learn from experience and enhance the value gained from using performance measures. A focus group needs to be selected from 15 to 30 experienced staff covering the business units, teams, area offices, head office. The staff will cover the different roles from administrators to senior management team members.

During the day the CSFs will be revisited, any new CSFs will be brainstormed for new measures, and the organizational measures will be reviewed for appropriateness and completeness.

Task 3. *Maintain the stakeholder consultation.* Ensure that consultations with stakeholders continue to be included in the performance review process. The stakeholders will provide feedback as to whether there needs to be improvement to strategies and CSFs.

Key suppliers should be consulted, as large operational efficiency can be achieved by vertical integration of systems. For example, one wood processor has online access to a major wood merchant's stock records. They are responsible for managing stock levels and delivering the timber. They send electronic invoices, trigger electronic payment, and update the stock system.

Task 4. *Allow team performance measures to adapt.* Maintaining the team's sense of ownership of performance measures is critical and will be achieved only if employees view performance measure information as valuable, useful, and worthwhile. As teams complete the process improvement cycle, KPI usefulness will be tested against new challenges to the team. Team performance measures must be adapted, as required, to maintain their relevance and use.

The checklist in Exhibit 3.29 can be used as an aid to the KPI project team, ensuring that important tasks are not overlooked. The KPI team, with the facilitator, should amend this checklist before use to suit the organization and the desired approach.

Benefits of This Step   The cycle of continuous improvement in the use of KPIs and PIs will be locked in place.

Exhibit 3.29   Refining and Modeling Checklist
(FS = step that links to a foundation stone)

1. Have the CSFs been reviewed as part of the strategic planning cycle?	❑ Yes ❑ No
2. Are organization-wide KPIs reviewed during the strategic planning cycle?	❑ Yes ❑ No
3. Does each team review their KPIs and PIs at least annually?	❑ Yes ❑ No
4. Are key customers informed when relevant *customer satisfaction* and *internal process* performance measures are modified?	❑ Yes ❑ No
5. Are key suppliers informed when relevant *internal process* performance measures are modified?	❑ Yes ❑ No
6. Have measures been put in place covering any vertical integration of systems with key customers and key suppliers?	❑ Yes ❑ No
7. Is there active continuing education to further develop staff and management understanding of KPIs?	❑ Yes ❑ No
8. Have new staff and management, particularly new members of the SMT, been educated about the benefits of "winning KPIs"?	❑ Yes ❑ No
9. Have stakeholders been consulted on any changes to the balanced scorecards? (FS)	❑ Yes ❑ No
10. Has there been an adequate transfer of knowledge from "performance management" experts to staff who will be introducing the new performance measures? (FS)	❑ Yes ❑ No

Exhibit 3.29   *(Continued)*

11. Have all proposed changes to measures, reports, and delegated authorities been carefully thought through? (FS)	❏ Yes ❏ No
12. Have the CSFs been reworked to reflect all changes to the strategies? (FS)	❏ Yes ❏ No
13. Are KRIs, PIs, and KPIs evolving over time?	❏ Yes ❏ No
14. Are rigorous controls and checks in place to ensure that changes to PIs and KPIs are genuine improvements?	❏ Yes ❏ No

Endnotes

1. *The KPI Manual,* 1996, now out of print.

2. Robert S. Kaplan and David P. Norton, *The Balanced Scorecard: Translating Strategy into Action.* Boston: Harvard Business School Press, 1996.

3. Ibid.

4. For additional information, see www.bettermanagement.com and look at the webcast by David Parmenter on "Quarterly Rolling Planning" and visit www.waymark.co.nz.

5. Jeremy Hope and Robin Fraser, *Beyond Budgeting: How Managers Can Break Free from the Annual Performance Trap.* Boston: Harvard Business School Press, 2003.

CHAPTER 4

KPI Team
Resource Kit

The key performance indicator (KPI) resource kit in this chapter is a companion guide for the successful development and use of KPIs in your organization.

It is essential that you work through this part of the book after you have read the introduction to winning KPIs and have viewed the general principles for the successful development and use of KPIs in Chapters 1 and 2, which explain the philosophy and process of introducing KPIs based on the practical experience of organizations pursuing better practice in this area.

The background information, general principles, associated guidelines, and case study material in Chapters 1 and 2 will all help you to use the resource kit.

USING THIS RESOURCE KIT

This resource kit assists the implementation of the 12 major steps set out in Chapter 3. The resource kit assumes that you will play a significant role in facilitating team development of winning KPIs.

The ideal way to use the resource kit is for the project team, the project team facilitator, managers, selected employees, and union delegates to work jointly through the 12 steps.

STEP 1 WORKSHEET: SENIOR MANAGEMENT TEAM COMMITMENT

The questionnaire in Exhibit 4.1 is for the senior management team (SMT) to complete. It will help the project team gauge the level of understanding within the SMT and thus provide useful information for marketing and educational initiatives directed at the SMT.

Half-Day Workshop for the SMT on Implementing KPIs—and Getting It Right the First Time

Workshop objectives:

- To ensure that the SMT are fully aware of what is required to implement performance measurement that works.
- To ensure that the SMT understand the required level of involvement, the necessity for speed, and the inherent hurdles performance measurement projects face
- To convey the difference between the organization's current performance measurement practices and one that links day-to-day activities to the strategic objectives

Requirements:

- Entire SMT to attend
- Pre-reading of KPI article
- Workshop administrator to help coordinate attendees
- One laptop, data show, screen, two electronic whiteboards, quiet workshop space away from the offices

Exhibit 4.1 Senior Management Team Commitment Questionnaire

The successful introduction of key performance indicators requires SMT commitment. Your feedback is appreciated.

Comments are an especially helpful part of the feedback process. Please take time to make comments as specific as possible and include examples where appropriate.

Please return **no later than** _____ by e-mail to _____

1. Have you worked with key performance indicators (KPIs) on a daily or weekly basis anytime in the past?	❏ Yes ❏ No
2. Do you understand the difference between critical success factors (CSFs), key result indicators (KRIs), performance indicators (PIs), and KPIs?	❏ Yes ❏ No
3. Are you prepared to delegate authority to teams so that they can take immediate action if KPIs go "off track"?	❏ Yes ❏ No
4. Are you prepared to set aside at least two hours a week for the next 16 weeks for interviews, reading progress reports, making decisions, providing input as required, etc.?	❏ Yes ❏ No
5. Would you be prepared to visit a "better practice" KPI organization?	❏ Yes ❏ No
6. Have you listened to the KPI presentation?	❏ Yes ❏ No
7. Are you prepared to attend a half-day workshop to kick-start the project?	❏ Yes ❏ No
8. Are you prepared to monitor on a daily basis (approximately 20 minutes a day) the eventual top five KPIs?	❏ Yes ❏ No

What are the three main ways the project team could help you maintain your commitment to this project?

Agenda:

8:00 A.M. Introduction by CEO.

8:10 A.M. The new thinking on KPIs:

- The difference between the three types of performance measures

- The characteristics of a winning KPI—two stories

- The 10/80/10 rule for performance measures

- Critical success factors (CSFs)

- Case studies

- Why so many performance measurement initiatives fail

- The difference between the organization's current performance measurement and that proposed

9:00 A.M. **Commence workshop 1:** Working with a couple of predetermined CSFs of the organization, perform a group brainstorming session on possible measures.

9:30 A.M. **Commence workshop 2:** In two groups, brainstorm the likely CSFs from a predetermined checklist. Each group looks at three balanced scorecard (BSC) perspectives.

10:00 A.M. Break.

10:15 A.M. **Recommence workshop 2:** Commence short-listing the CSFs to come up with five to eight CSFs, using relationship mapping.

11:00 A.M. **Commence workshop 3:** Brainstorm some performance measures for the organization (this task will take a further 10- to 16-week period to finalize).

108

11:40 A.M.   Short presentation on the way forward.

12:00 noon   Workshop ends.

One-Day Focus Group on Implementing Performance Measures—and Getting It Right the First Time

Objectives:

- To ensure a key group of staff and management are fully aware of what is required to implement performance measurement that works

- To fully understand the required level of involvement, the necessity for speed, and the inherent hurdles this project will face

Requirements:

- A focus group selected from 15 to 30 experienced staff members covering the business units, teams, area offices, and head office, and covering the different roles from administrators to SMT members

- Workshop administrator to help coordinate attendees

- At least three laptops, data show, screen, three electronic whiteboards, quiet workshop space away from the offices

Agenda:

9:00 A.M.   Introduction by CEO.

9:10 A.M.   The new thinking on key performance indicators presentation:

- The difference between the three types of performance measures

- The characteristics of a winning KPI—two stories

- The 10/80/10 rule for performance measures
- CSFs
- Case studies
- Why so many performance measurement initiatives fail
- The difference between the organization's current performance measurement and that proposed

All major budget holders are invited to join the focus group. Any SMT staff who missed the SMT workshop should attend this session. They leave after this session.

10:00 A.M.   **Commence workshop 1:** Brainstorming a collection of CSFs of the organization. All work that has already been done in this area will be tabled to attendees (e.g., CSFs from last few years' strategic plans).

10:30 A.M.   Break.

10:50 A.M.   **Recommence workshop 1:** Short-list the CSFs to come up with five to eight CSFs.

11:20 A.M.   **Commence workshop 2:** Design some key result indicators for the board (this task will take a further 10- to 16-week period to finalize).

12:00 noon   Lunch.

12:45 P.M.   **Commence workshop 3:** In different groups, brainstorm some performance measures for a couple of business units and a couple of selected teams (this task will take a further 10- to 16-week period to finalize for all business units and teams).

2:00 P.M.   Feedback from groups.

2:20 P.M.   Break.

2:40 P.M. **Commence workshop 4:** Brainstorm some performance measures for the organization (this task will take a further 10- to 16-week period to finalize).

3:40 P.M. Short presentation on the way forward—the implementation program.

4:20 P.M. In-house team complete workshop documentation on laptops (covering CSFs, some measures worth pursuing, the first draft of the next steps, resource requirements, etc.).

4:40 P.M. Focus group state their opinion on whether to go forward, the key issues to address, and resources required to the SMT.

SMT invited to come back to hear the focus group.

5:00 P.M. Workshop ends.

Progress Update Workshop for the SMT

Objective: To help maintain the interest of the SMT, gain valuable input, launch newly designed reports, and convey progress

Requirements:
- Entire SMT to attend
- Workshop administrator to help coordinate attendees
- One laptop, data show, screen, two electronic whiteboards, quiet workshop space away from the offices

Agenda:

8:00 A.M. Introduction by CEO.

8:10 A.M. Progress update.

9:00 A.M. **Commence workshop 1:** Perform exercises that will further the project.

10:00 A.M.   **Next steps.**

10:15 A.M.   Morning break and closure speech by CEO.

STEP 2 WORKSHEET: ESTABLISHING A WINNING KPI TEAM

The questionnaires in Exhibit 4.2 are to be completed by the proposed KPI team members and their peers and managers.

Exhibit 4.2   KPI Team Establishment Questionnaire

It is important that you answer these questions honestly so that any training gaps can be rectified quickly.

Comments are an especially helpful part of the feedback process. Please take time to make comments as specific as possible and include examples where appropriate.

Please return **no later than** _____ by e-mail to _____

1. Have you ever worked with key performance indicators (KPIs) on a daily or weekly basis?	❑ Yes ❑ No
2. Do you understand the difference between critical success factors (CSFs), key result indicators (KRIs), performance indicators (PIs), and KPIs?	❑ Yes ❑ No
3. Are you prepared to develop your skill base?	❑ Yes ❑ No
4. Are you prepared to set aside at least 16 weeks for interviews, site visits, liaison with facilitators and in-house coordinators, research, analysis, presenting findings, making recommends, etc.?	❑ Yes ❑ No
5. Have you had experience with:	
• "Post-It sticker reengineering"?	❑ Yes ❑ No
• Problem solving?	❑ Yes ❑ No
• Brainstorming?	❑ Yes ❑ No
• Information display and charting?	❑ Yes ❑ No
• Delivering presentations?	❑ Yes ❑ No

Exhibit 4.2 *(Continued)*

• Interviewing?	❑ Yes ❑ No
• Large implementation projects?	❑ Yes ❑ No
• Project management?	❑ Yes ❑ No
• The applications the project will use?	❑ Yes ❑ No
6. What is your skill base?	
• Are you a self-starter?	❑ Yes ❑ No
• Have you demonstrated innovation in the past?	❑ Yes ❑ No
• Have you advanced communication skills?	❑ Yes ❑ No
• Are you an "active" listener?	❑ Yes ❑ No
• Do you have the ability to bring others on board?	❑ Yes ❑ No
• Do you have a good track record in finishing projects you start?	❑ Yes ❑ No
• Are you able to maintain a big-picture focus while working on a project?	❑ Yes ❑ No
• Are you happy to work with the chosen facilitator?	❑ Yes ❑ No
• Are you happy to work with the chosen team members?	❑ Yes ❑ No
• Are you prepared to work overtime on this project to meet the time frames?	❑ Yes ❑ No

What are the three main strengths you bring to this project team?

What are the three main skill and experience gaps you have that need to be addressed before commencing this project?

Training gaps that are highlighted will need to be addressed before the project gains too much momentum.

Winning KPI Team Establishment Questionnaire

A small, well-trained project team has the best chance of success. It is recommended that a team of two to four people be chosen, who collectively have a wide range of skills, including: presentation, innovation, completion, knowledge of the organization and sector, communication, and the ability to bring others on board.

Winning KPI Team 360-Degree Questionnaire

Obtaining a 360-degree feedback on the short-listed team members will be most valuable in assessing their strengths and weaknesses. This questionnaire (Exhibit 4.3) should be completed by their manager and up to five of their peers with whom they work.

Exhibit 4.3   KPI Team 360-Degree Questionnaire

_____ has been short-listed for the team. It is important that you provide an unbiased response about _____'s experience and skills so that any training gaps can be rectified quickly.

Comments are an especially helpful part of the feedback process. Please take time to make comments as specific as possible and include examples where appropriate.

Please return **no later than** _____ by e-mail to _____

1. Are you prepared to release _____ for at least 16 weeks for the project?	❏ Yes ❏ No
2. Has _____ demonstrated problem-solving skills?	❏ Yes ❏ No
3. Has _____ demonstrated brainstorming skills?	❏ Yes ❏ No
4. Is _____ good at information display and charting?	❏ Yes ❏ No
5. Is _____ good at delivering thought-provoking presentations?	❏ Yes ❏ No

Exhibit 4.3 *(Continued)*

6. Does _____ have good interviewing skills?	❏ Yes	❏ No
7. Has _____ demonstrated project management skills?	❏ Yes	❏ No
8. Is _____ a self-starter?	❏ Yes	❏ No
9. Has _____ demonstrated innovation in the past?	❏ Yes	❏ No
10. Does _____ have advanced communication skills?	❏ Yes	❏ No
11. Is _____ an "active" listener?	❏ Yes	❏ No
12. Does _____ have the ability to bring others on board?	❏ Yes	❏ No
13. Does _____ have a good track record in finishing projects s/he starts?	❏ Yes	❏ No
14. Is _____ able to maintain a big-picture focus while working on a project?	❏ Yes	❏ No
15. Does _____ work overtime to meet agreed time frames?	❏ Yes	❏ No

What are the three main strengths _____ brings to this project team?

What are the three main skill and experience gaps _____ has that need to be addressed before commencing this project?

STEP 3 WORKSHEET: ESTABLISH A "JUST DO IT" CULTURE FOR THIS PROJECT

This worksheet is to help the team to do just that! The worksheet in Exhibit 4.4 should be completed by the project team.

Exhibit 4.4 Establish a "Just Do It" Culture Worksheet

1. Where will the key performance indicator (KPI) development process start? Will KPIs be introduced as a common program in all teams, or will some teams pilot the process so that they can then be a leadership resource?		
• All teams at once	❏ Yes	❏ No
• Pilot teams to lead the process	❏ Yes	❏ No
2. If pilots are to be used, the following criteria may help decide which teams to select. Desirable requirements for a successful pilot of team performance measures (performance indicators [PIs] and KPIs) include:		
• The pilot team(s) has been briefed and understands the organization-wide critical success factors (CSFs).	❏ Yes	❏ No
• The pilot team(s) has been trained to use this KPI book and the performance measure database.	❏ Yes	❏ No
• Pilot team members have already begun to exercise the authority that has been delegated to them.	❏ Yes	❏ No
• Pilot team members have been on a workshop to understand performance measures.	❏ Yes	❏ No
• The pilot team(s) can be easily supported by the KPI team.	❏ Yes	❏ No
• Pilot teams have a natural leader and function well under that leadership.	❏ Yes	❏ No
• Management is happy to delegate decision making to the team to allow corrective action when a KPI is off track.	❏ Yes	❏ No
3. What is the time frame for KPI introduction?	_____ Months	

Exhibit 4.4 *(Continued)*

4. What level of resource support is available to support the introduction of performance measures into teams?

_____

_____

_____

_____

_____

_____

_____

5. What type of approval or validation process is to be used to ensure that team performance measures are aligned with organization-wide CSFs?

• Teams are to work with all organizational CSFs.	❏ Yes ❏ No
• Database to record the CSFs the teams have finally selected.	❏ Yes ❏ No
_____	❏ Yes ❏ No
_____	❏ Yes ❏ No

6. Will an external facilitator (mentor) be available to help pilot teams develop their performance measures? ❏ Yes ❏ No

7. Will in-house facilitators be trained by the external facilitator to help? ❏ Yes ❏ No

8. Who has been identified to be trained as an in-house facilitator?

Name	Title	Location/Business Unit

(continues)

Exhibit 4.4   *(Continued)*

What three internal processes support a "just do it" culture?

What are the main three barriers to a "just do it" culture?

Supporting notes for Exhibit 4.4:

- *Question 1.* Change does not occur at a uniform pace. Some will embrace the concepts of partnership and empowerment before others. Early results from these teams should be marketed to those who are progressing at a slower rate.

  At least three criteria can be applied to assist selection of priority areas to pilot the introduction of winning KPIs and associated performance measures:

    1. *Acceptability.* Launch KPIs first in those teams that the SMT believe will be the most responsive to the concept and the process.
    2. *Urgency.* Launch KPIs in those teams that are responsible for key processes that require the most urgent performance improvement. Your key customers could help identify these areas.

3. *Consistency.* Launch performance measures in teams that need performance information to complement change strategies already under way. These include:

- ○ Self-managing teams
- ○ Customer-first program teams
- ○ Process improvement teams
- ○ Benchmarking teams.

- *Questions 2 to 5.* No notes required.
- *Question 6.* It is essential to use an external facilitator to bring alternative perspectives and expertise to both the winning KPI project team and the chosen pilots. While the KPI project team, once trained, can offer assistance to the pilot teams, it is important to avoid "the blind leading the blind."
- *Question 7.* The best in-house facilitators of the process are those team members displaying leadership within their team. In-house facilitators should be trained in KPI development, facilitation, training, and mentoring skills.

    In the spirit of partnership and empowerment, it may be appropriate to call for volunteers. This will depend on how successfully this method has been used in the past. When in doubt, use a targeted selection by management of the best-skilled facilitators, countering the resulting initial distrust with good communication and public relations.

STEP 4 WORKSHEET: SETTING UP A HOLISTIC KPI DEVELOPMENT STRATEGY

The worksheet in Exhibit 4.5 should be completed by the project team, having consulted widely with management who have been with the organization for some time, and been reviewed by selected members of the senior management team. Some gaps may appear, and additional documentation may be required by the strategic planning team. It is important that the KPI team does not get sidetracked into developing or refining the strategy—they just need to identify the gaps.

Exhibit 4.5   Holistic KPI Development Strategy Worksheet

1. Have any of the following been developed for your organization?	
• Vision statement	❑ Yes ❑ No
• Mission statement	❑ Yes ❑ No
• Strategic plan	❑ Yes ❑ No
• Identifying key strategies for achieving the vision	❑ Yes ❑ No
• Organizational values	❑ Yes ❑ No
2. To your knowledge, what are the formal, sanctioned change and improvement strategies or programs currently under way or planned for the next 12 months? (*Please list.*)	*Do these programs contain or require measurement to succeed?*
	❑ Yes ❑ No
	❑ Yes ❑ No
	❑ Yes ❑ No
	❑ Yes ❑ No
	❑ Yes ❑ No
	❑ Yes ❑ No
	❑ Yes ❑ No
	❑ Yes ❑ No
	❑ Yes ❑ No
3. Has your organization identified and agreed on a strategy for pursuing better practice?	❑ Yes ❑ No
4. Does a partnership between management, employees, and unions operate in relation to this strategy?	❑ Yes ❑ No

Exhibit 4.5 *(Continued)*

5. Which of these change and improvement strategies are organization-wide programs and which are local programs (i.e., specific to one division or area)?

Strategy or programs (from question 2)	Organization-wide	Local
_____	❏	❏
_____	❏	❏
_____	❏	❏
_____	❏	❏
_____	❏	❏
_____	❏	❏
_____	❏	❏
_____	❏	❏

6. Which of the following elements of better practice are currently in place within the organization?

• People practices	❏ Yes	❏ No
• Leadership	❏ Yes	❏ No
• Customer focus	❏ Yes	❏ No
• Quality of internal processes and outcomes	❏ Yes	❏ No
• Technological applications	❏ Yes	❏ No
• Organizational strategy	❏ Yes	❏ No
• Benchmarking	❏ Yes	❏ No

7. Consider whether the development of winning KPIs could be completed as part of the wider program, or be grafted onto education and training sessions associated with the wider program.

List strategies or programs (from question 2)	Part of the process	Additional to the process
_____	❏	❏
_____	❏	❏
_____	❏	❏
_____	❏	❏
_____	❏	❏
_____	❏	❏

(continues)

Exhibit 4.5 *(Continued)*

8. Taking into account all the change and improvement strategies in progress, can you answer "yes" to the following statements?	
• Senior management has already clarified, or is prepared to clarify, the critical success factors (CSFs) for the organization.	❏ Yes ❏ No
• Management accepts its obligation to adopt a consultative approach to the pursuit of better practice and the introduction of KPIs.	❏ Yes ❏ No
• Management is prepared to resource KPI development through training, provision of facilitators, and time off the job for employees.	❏ Yes ❏ No

Are there any key strategic issues that the project team should be aware of?

Supporting notes for Exhibit 4.5:

- *Question 1.* If you answered "No" to the existence of vision and mission statements or a strategic plan, it is advisable for a separate project team to address these elements. This team should communicate regularly with the KPI team. While the development of strategic direction requires senior management involvement, consultation with employees and customers is highly beneficial.

  Organizations are waking up to the fact that this linkage must be understood if staff are to be "fast, focused, and flexible" as Bruce Holland, a well-known strategic planner and communicator, puts it. Strategic planning processes must be much more inclusive if your organization is to reap benefits.

Holland says, "If you have done your job properly, you should be able to rip up the final document, as staff and management have the linkage imprinted in their memory." Achieving this level of understanding is much quicker and easier than most managers and CEOs believe. Getting people throughout the organization involved can generate high levels of understanding, energy, goodwill, and commitment.

Understanding the difference between a mission, values, vision, and strategy is vital. The *mission* is like a timeless "beacon" that may never be reached (e.g., Walt Disney, "to make people happy"; 3M, "to solve unsolved problems innovatively").

The *values* are what your organization stands for "we believe . . ." (e.g., a public-sector entity has the values "seek innovation and excellence, engage constructively, ask questions, support and help each other, bring solutions, see the bigger picture").

The *vision* is where the organization wants to go in a defined time frame. The vision is the tool to galvanize your organization if it is stated with enough clarity and commitment and will change over time. Some are famous, for example, John F. Kennedy's statement, "I believe that this nation should commit itself to achieving the goal, before this decade is out, of landing a man on the moon and returning him safely to the earth."

This simple statement galvanized the entire U.S. scientific community to a herculean effort. Every day, week, and month, employees around the United States worked toward this vision. From the moment it was stated, NASA experts began to plan how the millions of building blocks required were to be put together.

Strategy is the way an organization intends to achieve its vision. In a competitive environment, your strategy will distinguish you from your competition. Within the public sector, your strategy is the way you can best marshal your resources to achieve desired outcomes.

If you answered "yes" to the existence of vision and mission statements or a strategic plan, you will need to obtain those documents and possibly approval for the release of the information contained in them to all the organization's employees. For any information that is deemed too sensitive for release due to market competition, sensitive information will need to be redrafted to allow communication to employees.

If you answered "yes" to the existence of a set of organizational values, you should review these to identify the behavioral standards your organization is promoting in relation to:

- Access to information
- Communication and consultation processes
- The introduction of change

You must keep these behavioral standards in mind as you develop KPIs (following the 12 steps) to ensure that the process aligns with the organization's stated values.

- *Question 2.* Depending on your location and position in the organization, you may need to consult widely to develop this list. Most large organizations will have a number of change and improvement strategies under way or planned at any given time.

  Some of these programs will incorporate their own specific measurement strategy (e.g., occupational health and safety systems or materials resource planning). Other programs (such as process improvement teams or self-managing teams) will often not contain a prescriptive measurement approach as part of the implementation package, even though they require measurement to succeed.

- *Question 3.* For a change process to succeed, there needs to be a holistic strategy for achieving performance improvement that is developed, agreed to, and shared by management and its employees or their representatives.

- *Question 4.* Much of what follows relies on this partnership's being in place. If you cannot answer "yes" to question 4, some major wide-ranging consultation is recommended before KPI development is pursued.

- *Question 5.* Some local programs may warrant organizational rollout especially if they support the KPI process.

- *Question 6.* Better practice suggests that world-class performance levels are achieved only when all of the elements of better practice are in place.

    If you answered "no" to the presence of any specific element of best practice, it may be wise to complete the gaps in your organization's strategy. Filling these gaps can be achieved in conjunction with the KPI development process.

- *Question 7.* For example, a program to achieve quality accreditation could be broadened to include the development of KPIs. Similarly, education and training sessions associated with a "Customer First" program could be extended to include the development of KPIs.

- *Question 8.* You need three "yes" responses to be able to commence a change strategy, based on partnership, designed to achieve best practice. If you are unable to achieve three "yes" responses, it may be advisable to review the general principles in Chapter 1.

STEP 5 WORKSHEET: MARKETING THE KPI SYSTEM TO ALL EMPLOYEES

A formal briefing program is to be held to outline the changes associated with introducing KPIs into the organization. By its conclusion all employees should at least believe that they need to do something differently, and a core group should be clear about implementation issues and how performance measures will be used.

Before you can explain the concept, you need to ascertain the level of understanding among all staff. This is best achieved through a survey. It is important to survey the SMT, middle managers or supervisors, and employees and record their responses to these questions.

Marketing KPIs to All Employees Questionnaire

With the help of the human resources team, make a selection of experienced staff covering all regions, levels of staff, and so forth. This sample should not be greater than 200, less than 30, or larger than 5% of total staff. Too large a sample will make data mining more difficult and seldom raise any new issues. See Exhibit 4.6.

Exhibit 4.6   Employee Questionnaire

The comment fields are a useful part of the feedback process. Please take time to make comments as specific as possible and provide examples where appropriate.

Please return **no later than** _____ by e-mail to _____

Please mark your response in the appropriate column: SMT = senior management team, MM&S = middle management and supervisors, S = staff.

Existing performance information in the organization is:	SMT		MM&S		S	
• Well understood	❏ Yes	❏ No	❏ Yes	❏ No	❏ Yes	❏ No
• Easily obtainable	❏ Yes	❏ No	❏ Yes	❏ No	❏ Yes	❏ No
• Used to aid improvement	❏ Yes	❏ No	❏ Yes	❏ No	❏ Yes	❏ No
• Thought to be used to allocate blame	❏ Yes	❏ No	❏ Yes	❏ No	❏ Yes	❏ No
• Regarded as accurate/credible	❏ Yes	❏ No	❏ Yes	❏ No	❏ Yes	❏ No
• Regularly reviewed in a formal manner	❏ Yes	❏ No	❏ Yes	❏ No	❏ Yes	❏ No

Exhibit 4.6 *(Continued)*

What do you think will be the three main issues of concern to employees with the introduction of KPIs?

What are the three main issues that should be addressed in initial employee briefings?

What are the three most important ways in which the SMT can assist marketing KPIs throughout the organization?

Complete the worksheet in Exhibit 4.7 to ensure that all staff concerns have been addressed. Supporting notes for Exhibits 4.6 and 4.7 follow:

- **Employee questionnaire (Exhibit 4.6).** This question assesses current understanding of the purpose and use of performance information. Generally, the more "no" responses, the bigger the

Exhibit 4.7 Identifying Employee Concerns about Performance Measurement Worksheet

1. For each concern identified, indicate how it is to be addressed

Area of employee concern	Making definite commitments about the use of KPIs	Highlighting employees' roles in the development and implementation process

2. How many employees need to be briefed about KPIs?   _____ employees

What percentage of employees who need to be briefed have:

- Limited levels of English language comprehension?   ____ %
- A low level of literacy?   ____ %
- A low level of numeracy?   ____ %

3. How should these briefings be conducted?

	Group 1	Group 2	Group 3	Group 4
Person giving the briefing				
Size of groups				
Time allocated				
Locations				
Proposed dates				

educational task ahead. The answer "yes" to the question "Existing performance information is thought to be used to allocate blame" provides insight into the current measurement culture.

The responses to "What are the three main issues that should be addressed in initial employee briefings?" will highlight issues that will need to be raised during initial employee briefings. These may include:

- **Why KPIs are being introduced.** Discuss the organization's current position, competitive/external pressures, and future direction. Explain how KPIs assist in achieving the desired future direction.

- **How KPIs will be developed.** Stress the points at which employee involvement, training, and consultation will take place.

- **How KPIs will be used.** Emphasize team and work group use to achieve performance improvement.

- **What KPIs will not be used for.** Develop a list, addressing employee concerns, of what KPIs will not be used for (e.g., to reduce workforce size or discipline individuals).

- **Worksheet (Exhibit 4.7).** This worksheet addresses language, literacy, and numeracy issues in KPI briefings for employees.

  In the longer term, your organization may need to consider specific programs to address the language, literacy, and numeracy needs of its employees.

  If you have significant numbers of employees with these three characteristics, your initial briefing strategy (and your later KPI development process at the team level) will need to be tailored to meet their particular requirements.

  In the short term, there are two options to help overcome these potential barriers to KPI development and use:

  1. *English language barriers.* Generally, most non-English language–speaking groups within an organization rely

on those in their group with the highest level of English comprehension to act as translators. Therefore, to achieve effective understanding of the purpose and use of KPIs, you will need to direct briefings toward those bilingual employees. These employees will then need to receive assistance in briefing the employees in their language group.

2. *Literacy and numeracy barriers.* The sensitivity of these issues means it is generally not wise to highlight those affected. However, reasonable comprehension can be achieved by all if groups are structured so that such employees are not grouped together. Additional time should be allocated in all briefing sessions for discussion in small groups to allow these employees to confirm their understanding.

Road Show for Staff—and Getting It Right First Time

Objectives:

- To ensure that staff are fully aware of what is required to implement performance measurement that works
- To fully understand the inherent hurdles this project will face from the staff's point of view

Requirements:

- Workshop administrator to help coordinate attendees
- At least three laptops, data show, screen, three electronic whiteboards, quiet workshop space away from the offices

Agenda:

9:00 A.M.   Introduction from local management.

9:10 A.M.   Video is shown; the content would include:

- Introduction by CEO
- The new thinking on key performance indicators (KPIs) presentation, presented by a skilled presenter from the project team:
  - The difference between the three types of performance measures
  - The characteristics of a winning KPI—two stories
  - The 10/80/10 rule for performance measures
  - Critical success factors (CSFs) for the organization
  - Working through how to brainstorm performance measures
  - Why so many BSCs fail
  - The implementation program
  - How these new performance measures will affect your day-to-day activities

9:50 A.M.   **Commence workshop 1, which will be facilitated by a trained business unit or team coordinator:** Brainstorm as one large group the team performance measures in one perspective (suggest learning and growth, as it will be generic for most teams)

10:10 A.M.   **Commence workshop 2:** In different groups, brainstorm team performance measures, short-listing the performance measures to come up with 15 to 25 measures (this task will take a further 10- to 16-week period to finalize for all business units and teams)

10:30 A.M.   Break.

10:50 A.M.   **Recommence workshop 2.**

11:20 A.M. **Commence workshop 3:** What are the hurdles this project needs to deal with, and what delegated authority needs to be put in place?

12:00 noon Feedback from groups and a common understanding is reached on the hurdles and the best way around them and what delegated authority needs to be given.

12:30 P.M. Conclusion and lunch.

STEP 6 WORKSHEET: IDENTIFYING ORGANIZATION-WIDE CSFs

The worksheet in Exhibit 4.8 assists with the location and identification of the organization-wide CSFs. This worksheet should be completed by the project team.

Exhibit 4.8   Identifying Organization-Wide CSFs Worksheet

1. Have critical success factors (CSFs) been defined for your organization?	❑ Yes ❑ No
2. If so, have they been recently reviewed to confirm relevance?	❑ Yes ❑ No
List your organization's current CSFs and indicate if they make the top eight CSFs.	**In top 8 CSFs**
	❑ Yes ❑ No
	❑ Yes ❑ No
	❑ Yes ❑ No
	❑ Yes ❑ No
	❑ Yes ❑ No
	❑ Yes ❑ No
	❑ Yes ❑ No
	❑ Yes ❑ No

Exhibit 4.8   *(Continued)*

3. List possible additional CSFs that will require investigation for relevance.

4. How do your top eight CSFs cover the six perspectives of performance?

Critical Success Factor	Financial	Customer Satisfaction	Staff Satisfaction	Learning and Growth	Internal Process	Environment/ Community
E.g., timely arrival and departure of planes	✓	✓	✓	✓	✓	Possible
E.g., delivery in full and on time	✓	✓	Possible	✓	✓	
1.		✓			✓	✓
2.	✓					
3.						
4.						
5.						
6.						
7.						
8.						

5. Have the top eight CSFs been discussed with employee representatives?   ❏ Yes   ❏ No

(continues)

133

Exhibit 4.8 *(Continued)*

6. Do the top eight CSFs cover the following issues?		
CSF for environment/community		
Supporting minorities through employment	❑ Yes	❑ No
Minimizing pollution (waste management)	❑ Yes	❑ No
Support educational institutions (share knowledge via organization's website)	❑ Yes	❑ No
Encouraging voluntary assistance by staff to local community	❑ Yes	❑ No
Recognition by industry for environmental endeavors	❑ Yes	❑ No
Good working relationships with key community organizations		
Supporting local businesses (% of purchases to have local content)	❑ Yes	❑ No
Enhanced community interaction (favorable reputation in the community, seen as an employer of choice)	❑ Yes	❑ No
Environmentally friendly culture and reputation (use of environmentally friendly materials, support of "green globe" initiatives	❑ Yes	❑ No
Positive public perception of organization	❑ Yes	❑ No
CSF for internal process		
Product leadership in industry	❑ Yes	❑ No
Safe and healthy workplace	❑ Yes	❑ No
Enhancing operational efficiency, reducing cost per transaction	❑ Yes	❑ No
Increased linkages with key suppliers	❑ Yes	❑ No
Optimizing technology	❑ Yes	❑ No
Completion on time and to budget measure	❑ Yes	❑ No
Encouraging innovation	❑ Yes	❑ No
Enhancing quality	❑ Yes	❑ No
Constantly adopting ways to work smarter (accurate and timely processing of transactions, continuous improvement in key processes)	❑ Yes	❑ No
Occupational health and safety legislation compliance	❑ Yes	❑ No

Exhibit 4.8 *(Continued)*

CSF for internal process *(continued)*	
Timely, accurate, decision-based information	❏ Yes ❏ No
Successful completion of projects (we finish what we start)	❏ Yes ❏ No
Timely maintenance of assets	❏ Yes ❏ No
Effective relationships with key stakeholders	❏ Yes ❏ No
Delivery in full on time, all the time	❏ Yes ❏ No
CSF for finance	
Optimizing revenue from profitable customers	❏ Yes ❏ No
Growth in revenue and product mix (new products, new applications, new customers and markets, new relationships, new product and service mix, new pricing)	❏ Yes ❏ No
Cost reduction/productivity improvement (reduce unit cost, improve channel mix, reduce operating expenses)	❏ Yes ❏ No
Increasing the gross margin	❏ Yes ❏ No
Optimal utilization of assets and resources	❏ Yes ❏ No
Improved risk management (better forecasting, broaden revenue base, etc.)	❏ Yes ❏ No
Increase in overall spend by core customers (getting a larger slice of business from our important customers)	❏ Yes ❏ No
Increased repeat business (leading to increasing market share)	❏ Yes ❏ No
Optimization of working capital (optimizing stock levels and minimizing debtors)	❏ Yes ❏ No
Fiscally responsible management	❏ Yes ❏ No
Improving cash flow	❏ Yes ❏ No
Maximizing off-season potential	❏ Yes ❏ No
Being a preferred supplier for main customers (more success at tenders, more nontender opportunities)	❏ Yes ❏ No
Recovery of chargeable hours	❏ Yes ❏ No

(continues)

Exhibit 4.8   *(Continued)*

CSF for customer		
Introduction of new services	❑ Yes	❑ No
Moving from satisfied to loyal customers (increasing the number of customer referrals, meeting customer expectations in full)	❑ Yes	❑ No
Customer acquisition	❑ Yes	❑ No
Increased satisfaction with our key customers (timely service, reliability, quality, price)	❑ Yes	❑ No
Improving turnaround time of _____	❑ Yes	❑ No
Increased repeat business (increased percentage of sales from key customers)	❑ Yes	❑ No
Ensuring delivery in full on time, all the time for key customers	❑ Yes	❑ No
Retention of key customers (e.g., smart partnership programs, rewards, etc.)	❑ Yes	❑ No
Positive brand recognition	❑ Yes	❑ No
CSF for learning and growth		
Developing internal leadership	❑ Yes	❑ No
Increasing employee productivity	❑ Yes	❑ No
Developing strategic skills within management	❑ Yes	❑ No
Increase in adaptability and flexibility of staff	❑ Yes	❑ No
More open access for staff to strategic information	❑ Yes	❑ No
Improved alignment of individual and organizational goals	❑ Yes	❑ No
Increase in empowerment (delegated decision making)	❑ Yes	❑ No
Increase in productivity through increase in skills, motivation, etc.	❑ Yes	❑ No
Multifaceted support to employees' growth (coaching, mentoring, managed by skilled managers, succession planning, project opportunities)	❑ Yes	❑ No
Research and development and knowledge rewarded and encouraged	❑ Yes	❑ No

Exhibit 4.8   *(Continued)*

CSF for employee satisfaction		
Retention of key staff	❏ Yes	❏ No
Increase in employee satisfaction	❏ Yes	❏ No
Positive company culture (supported by staff satisfaction survey, active and well-supported social club, etc.)	❏ Yes	❏ No
Providing opportunities for staff to grow	❏ Yes	❏ No
Supporting balanced working and nonworking life (respect different working styles/working hours)	❏ Yes	❏ No
Appropriate reward and recognition structure for all	❏ Yes	❏ No
Continuous learning environment	❏ Yes	❏ No
Promoting open decision making	❏ Yes	❏ No
Increased recognition (celebrating success)	❏ Yes	❏ No
A pleasant physical work environment for all staff	❏ Yes	❏ No

Supporting notes for Exhibit 4.8:

- *Question 1.* If your strategic plan does not currently define CSFs or key result areas (KRAs), you will need to develop them from the information contained in the plan.

- *Question 2.* General principles indicate that a better practice approach to identification of CSFs or KRAs involves identifying factors related to organizational performance. As a guide, ensure that CSFs are nominated in the following areas:

  - Customer focus (service and satisfaction)
  - Financial performance
  - Learning and growth (human resource development, workforce contribution and involvement)
  - Internal processes (including innovation, operational efficiency, measurement, reporting, use of technology, etc.)

- ○ Employee satisfaction
- ○ Environment/community
- *Question 3.* No note required
- *Question 4.* CSFs will be sourced from existing documentation, brainstorming, and interviews with the SMT and "oracles." To find your five to eight CSFs, a good technique is to draw all your CSFs on a large whiteboard and draw in all the linkages. The CSFs with the most linkages are the more important ones. Other techniques are:
  - ○ Using weightings asking those in the workshop to score their top CSFs from 8 (highest) to 1 (lowest). The top eight CSFs will be the highest scoring ones.
  - ○ Using strategy mapping if you have the software which can be sourced from balanced scorecard collaborative, and so on.

  Exhibit 4.9 provides an example of how you use relationship maps on a whiteboard to work out which CSFs are in the top eight.

  Some organizations from the original studies found it useful to do process mapping at this stage. However, process maps often consume a lot of resources and can become so complex that only those documenting them understand or have the enthusiasm to try to follow them.

- *Question 5.* If answered "no," the performance measure development process needs to be put on hold. In effect, there is no agreement as to the direction in which the organization is going. It is also likely that there is not sufficient agreement on the holistic strategy for achieving best practice.

  Without this agreement, the principle of partnership cannot be met. The only option is to consult further to secure agreement.

  CSF selection must ensure that all those factors critical for organizational success are taken into account. For example,

Exhibit 4.9 Relationship Mapping CSFs on a Whiteboard

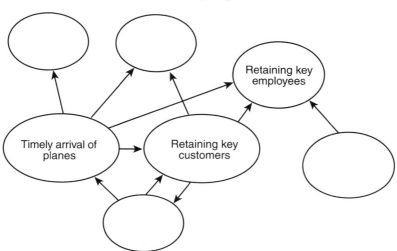

financial performance is an obvious CSF, regardless of the sector or market. Performance in non-financial areas can, however, prove just as critical for current and future organizational success.

You will need to run a workshop to find the CSFs. Some exercises are provided in Exhibit 4.10.

Exhibit 4.10 Determining the CSFs Workshop Exercises

Workshop: Revisiting Your Organization's Critical Success Factors

Learning Outcome:

Short-list the organization's critical success factors (CSFs).

Understand the importance of CSFs in targeting performance measures.

Steps	Time
1. Working in teams, work on one or two perspectives, remembering that you are focusing on the organization as a whole and business unit CSFs may be slightly different.	

(continues)

Exhibit 4.10 *(Continued)*

Steps	Time
2. Select a chairperson, whose role is to ensure that everyone understands the outcome, understands the instructions, and has an opportunity to contribute.	
3. Brainstorm the likely CSFs in the perspectives you have been assigned.	1 hour
4. Now compare the CSFs in the checklist to the ones you have come up with. Are there any missing? Include those that you believe are now relevant.	10 mins
5. Using relationship mapping or strategic mapping, work out which CSFs are the most important in that perspective.	40 mins
6. Gather back all teams. Each group reports back on the top three CSFs in the perspectives they were working in.	5 mins for each group
7. Notice the CSFs that have arisen in different perspectives (these are a sign of being more important) and short-list to the top three in each perspective (there will be repeats).	30 mins
8. Using relationship mapping or strategic mapping with this short list (max of 18, e.g., 6 perspectives, 3 CSFs each), work out which are the five to eight CSFs that are the most important.	1 hour

STEP 7 WORKSHEET: COMPREHENSIVE RECORDING OF MEASURES WITHIN THE DATABASE

The project team should complete the worksheet in Exhibit 4.11 to ensure all information required is captured in the database.

STEP 8 WORKSHEET: SELECTING TEAM PERFORMANCE MEASURES

This step contains three discrete activities, which should be performed in a workshop led by the project team or by an external facilitator. These activities are:

140

Exhibit 4.11 Ensure Comprehensive Recording
Performance Measures Worksheet

Check that there is a field in the database for each of the following:		
• Name of performance measure	❏ Yes	❏ No
• Calculation of measure	❏ Yes	❏ No
• Type of performance measure, key results indicator (KRI), performance indicator (PI), key performance indicator (KPI)	❏ Yes	❏ No
• Person responsible	❏ Yes	❏ No
• System in which data is going to be gathered	❏ Yes	❏ No
• Balanced scorecard (BSC) perspective	❏ Yes	❏ No
• Recommended display (e.g., type of graph)	❏ Yes	❏ No
• Frequency of measurement (24/7, daily, weekly, monthly)	❏ Yes	❏ No
• Link to critical success factors (CSFs)	❏ Yes	❏ No
• Teams interested in using measure	❏ Yes	❏ No
• Suggested performance target (this can be ranged and get tougher over time), for example, 30–40 or 25–30 by end 200X	❏ Yes	❏ No
• Required reliability/accuracy (±5%, ±10%, ±20%)	❏ Yes	❏ No
• Estimated time to gather information (15 mins, 30 mins, 1 hour, ½ day, 1 day, > 1day)	❏ Yes	❏ No
• Implementation issues	❏ Yes	❏ No
• Training required to collect data	❏ Yes	❏ No

Activity 1 Gaining an effective understanding of the organization's CSFs

Activity 2 Identifying the major internal processes to focus on and therefore measure

Activity 3   Selecting team performance measures and confirming their suitability for collection and use

These team members should be supported either by members of the KPI team or by the external facilitator. It is important that the facilitator is skilled at running workshops.

The worksheets in Exhibits 4.12 and 4.13 should be completed by the members of teams who are looking at their performance measures as a part of this project. Exhibit 4.14 provides the worksheet for selecting team performances and confirming suitability.

To determine whether a particular performance measure is worth collecting, the team should consider the following:

- Time spent on collection, collation, and analysis compared to the value of results obtained from this information

- Level of data accuracy (can we achieve consistent accuracy? Will the team make decisions based on this information?)

- Timeliness of the data (Will information become available in sufficient time to allow appropriate action?)

You will need to hold team balanced scorecard workshops; some workshop exercises are provided in Exhibit 4.15.

STEP 9 WORKSHEET: SELECTING ORGANIZATION-WIDE "WINNING KPIs"

The worksheet in Exhibit 4.16 should be completed by the KPI project team.

In order to finalize the KRIs to be reported to the board, you will need to hold a workshop with some members of the original focus group. See the workshop outline in Exhibit 4.17.

Exhibit 4.12 Activity 1 Worksheet: Gaining an Effective
Understanding of the Organization's CSFs

1. What do we mean by critical success factors (CSFs)? Think about
your own personal health and well-being. What are the major factors that
determine how long we live and the physical quality of life we enjoy (e.g.,
condition of heart, condition of lungs)?

| |
| |
| |
| |
| |
| |

2. In the same way, the CSFs for our organization are about the things that
determine its health and long-term survival. Here are our organization's
CSFs and which perspective they affect.

Critical Success Factor	Financial	Customer Satisfaction	Staff Satisfaction	Learning and Growth	Internal Process	Environment/ Community
E.g., timely arrival and departure of planes	✓	✓	✓	✓	✓	Possible
E.g., delivery in full and on time	✓	✓	Possible	✓	✓	
1.		✓			✓	✓
2.	✓					
3.						
4.						
5.						
6.						
7.						
8.						

Discuss these CSFs and consider why they affect your organization's health.

(continues)

143

Exhibit 4.12   *(Continued)*

3. Can you see why each CSF was selected?	❑ Yes ❑ No

4. In your opinion, why do we need performance measures?

5. Think about your personal health again. If there are a few CSFs that determine our health, how would we measure these?

CSF	Measure
E.g., condition of heart	E.g., blood pressure measured daily, cholesterol test every three months, chart of cholesterol results over last three years
E.g., condition of lungs	E.g., lung test every year, how many exercise sessions are planned this week, how many achieved this week so far?

6. Does measuring these critical factors help us to manage our personal health?	❑ Yes ❑ No
7. Do you have any additional questions about CSFs and performance measures?	❑ Yes ❑ No

Question

Exhibit 4.12 *(Continued)*

8. How can the project team help your team develop their performance measures?

Exhibit 4.13 Activity 2 Worksheet: Identifying Major Internal Processes Your Team Should Focus On

List your major processes			
Process	**Generate product or service delivery to customers**	**Cause most problem**	**Negative impact on team**
	❑	❑	❑
	❑	❑	❑
	❑	❑	❑
	❑	❑	❑
	❑	❑	❑
	❑	❑	❑
	❑	❑	❑
	❑	❑	❑
	❑	❑	❑
	❑	❑	❑
	❑	❑	❑
	❑	❑	❑
	❑	❑	❑

Exhibit 4.14   Activity 3 Worksheet: Selecting Team Performances
and Measures and Confirming Suitability

1. For each critical success factor (CSF) listed, develop some performance
measures for your team using this worksheet. The brainstorming sessions
can be documented on a computerized mind-map (freeware).

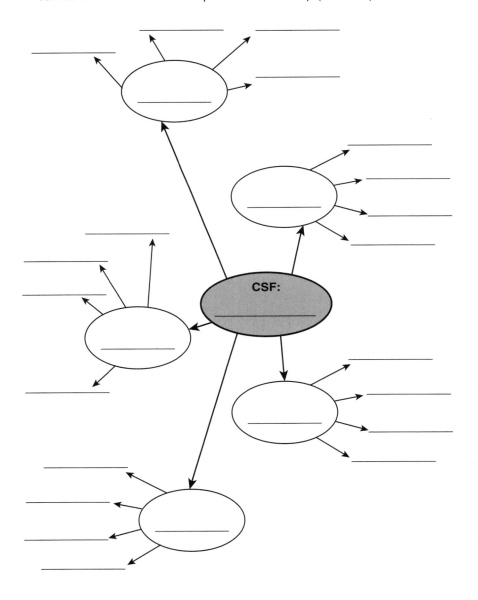

Exhibit 4.14 (Continued)

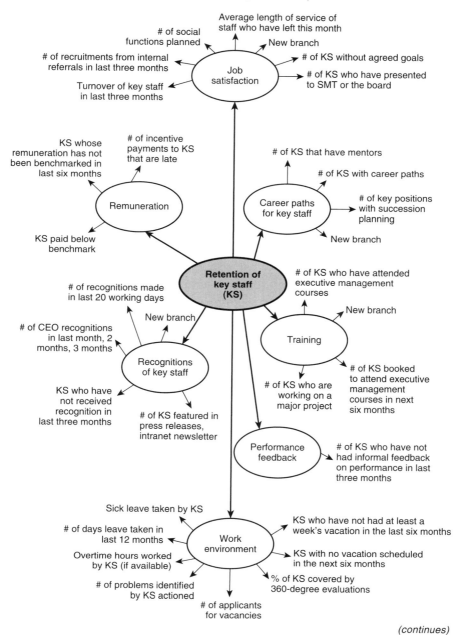

Exhibit 4.14 *(Continued)*

2. Confirming availability of information. For each performance measure, answer the following:

Possible performance measure	Who collects it and how frequently?	Is it cost effective to collect?
		❑ Yes ❑ No
		❑ Yes ❑ No
		❑ Yes ❑ No
		❑ Yes ❑ No
		❑ Yes ❑ No
		❑ Yes ❑ No
		❑ Yes ❑ No
		❑ Yes ❑ No

3. If the information required is not already available, could it be developed, and if so is it worth the effort?

Possible performance measure where data is not available (from Step 2)	How would it be collected?

Exhibit 4.15   Team Balanced Scorecards Workshop Exercises

Workshop 1: Workshop together the performance measures that a team may have for *employee satisfaction* and *learning and growth* perspectives

Learning Outcome: Learn how to brainstorm a balanced scorecard perspective for a team

Steps	Time
1. Working together, use a mind-map to brainstorm the employee satisfaction and learning and growth perspectives; remember, there is not a bad suggestion!	20 minutes
2. Fine-tune the suggestions and find relevant measures; remember, you need some current and future measures.	20 minutes

Workshop 2: Developing team performance measures

Learning Outcome: Develop and refine your likely performance measures

Steps	Time
1. Select a chairperson, whose role is to ensure that everyone understands the outcome, understands the instructions, and has an opportunity to contribute.	
2. Working in teams, use a mind-map to brainstorm the two perspectives you have been given: • Group 1 discusses team *financial and internal process measures.* • Group 2 discusses team *financial and internal process measures.* • Group 3 discusses team *environment/community and customer focus measures.* • Group 4 discusses team *environment/community and customer focus measures.*	1 hour
3. Use a mind-map and work together.	
4. Each group reports back on their measures; discuss only those that have already been raised.	5 minutes for each group

(continues)

149

Exhibit 4.15 *(Continued)*

Workshop 3: Reviewing performance indicators checklist for other measures

Learning Outcome: Refine your team scorecard

Steps	Time
1. Working by yourself, review the measures we have discussed and fine-tune your scorecard.	10 minutes
2. Clean your scorecard; take care in removing rows!	10 minutes
3. Present your scorecard to the group, covering the measures that have not already been discussed.	5 minutes for each scorecard

Exhibit 4.16   Selecting Organization-Wide "Winning KPIs" Worksheet

1. Have up to ten KPIs been identified (less is better than more)?	❏ Yes	❏ No
2. Have all KPIs been linked to strategy?	❏ Yes	❏ No
3. Have all KPIs been included in team performance measures?	❏ Yes	❏ No
4. Are all KPIs understood by all team members?	❏ Yes	❏ No
5. Has the KPI check been performed on all KPIs?	❏ Yes	❏ No
6. Have checks been made to ensure that KPIs do not include KRIs or performance indicators?	❏ Yes	❏ No
7. Have simple systems been established to report movement in KPIs as they occur?	❏ Yes	❏ No
8. Have all perspectives been covered by the KPIs?	❏ Yes	❏ No

KPI Checklist

KPI checklist of characteristics	Insert KPI name at the top of each column								
Nonfinancial measures (not expressed in dollars, yen, pounds, euros, etc.)									

Exhibit 4.16   *(Continued)*

KPI checklist of characteristics *(continued)*	Insert KPI name at the top of each column									
Measured frequently (e.g., weekly, daily, or 24/7)										
Acted on by CEO and senior management team										
All staff understand the measure and what corrective action is required										
Responsibility can be tied to the individual or team										
Significant impact (e.g., it impacts most of the core critical success factors [CSFs] and more than one balanced scorecard perspective)										
Has a positive impact (e.g., affects all other performance measures in a positive way)										

STEP 10 WORKSHEET: DEVELOPING DISPLAY, REPORTING, AND REVIEW FRAMEWORKS AT ALL LEVELS

The project team should complete this worksheet to ensure that measures are reported using appropriate templates (see Exhibits 4.18 and 4.19). An example of a completed team scorecard is set out in Exhibit 4.18.

Exhibit 4.17   Designing a Dashboard for the Board with KRIs Worksheet

Learning Outcome: Develop a performance measure report for the board

Steps	Time
1. Select the chairperson, whose role is to ensure that everyone understands the outcome, understands the instructions, and has an opportunity to contribute.	
2. Review the output from the earlier focus group workshops.	20 minutes
3. Working with your allocated perspectives and the CSFs you have already developed, discuss the likely KRIs within these CSFs.	1 hour
4. Design a graph for each KRI you have come up with. *One person* in each work group is to draw the graphs carefully, as these will be photocopied and viewed by other groups.	20 minutes
5. Each group reports back on their suggested graphs (once photocopies have been returned).	10 minutes for each group

Exhibit 4.19 presents the worksheet for setting team goals. This worksheet should be completed by each team.

STEP 11 WORKSHEET: FACILITATING THE USE OF KPIs

The road show is run by a local facilitator who has been trained by the KPI team.

The use of a video is important because the CEO will not be able to get around to all units in the required time. See Exhibit 4.20 for an outline for a video road show.

Exhibit 4.18 Team Scorecard and a Draft for Completion; Developing Display, Reporting, and Review Frameworks at All Levels Worksheet Example (performance measures should be reported in a team scorecard)

Balanced scorecard for the Finance function
As of September 30, 2007

Customer focus

Customer focused initiatives	This month	Target
Accounting system downtime (8am-6pm)	30mins	<60mins
Last update of intranet page	1/08/07	weekly
Service requests outstanding	24	15
Service requests closed in month	8 (40%)	60%
Programmed visits to budget holders	4	6
P&P updated on the intranet	0	1
Initiatives underway based on satisfaction survey	2	4

Usage of G/L by management	This month	Target
Managers accessing the G/L (#)	2	10
Managers accessing the G/L (time)	30 mins	2 hours
Suppliers on A/P	600	400

Project status

Xxxxx / Matrix / Xxxxx / Xxxxx / Xxxxx / Budget system / Balanced scorecard / Grants system / Revenue forecast — 0% 20% 40% 60% 80% 100%

☑ Done ☐ On-Track ☑ Behind ■ Risk of Non-Completion

Delivery

Efficiency measures	This month	Target
Report to budget holders	2	By day 2
Report to Xxxxx	3	By day 3
Finance report to Xxxxx	4	By day 4
% of payments made by direct credit	80%	>75%
# of strategic supply relationships	1	4
# of accounts paid late	12	<20
# of customer calls in test week	15	<20
% of invoices issued on time	90%	99%
Projects completed on time on budget	44%	80%

Completions	Current	Target
Projects in progress	9	<8
Reports/documents still in draft mode	10	<5

Learning and growth

Training needs outstanding	This month	YTD
CFO	0	2
Finance	0	5
Mngt Accounting	0	3
A/P team	0	2
A/R team	1	2
Average for all accounting staff	n/a	2.5

Post project reviews	current	target
Post project reviews undertaken to ascertain lessons learnt	0	4

Performance reviews	current	target
Staff who have had 2 performance reviews in the last year	10	23

Financial

% spent of this year's capital expenditure

Accounting function expenditure profile

—♦— Planned Cumulative   —■— Forecast Cumulative   —▲— Actual Cumulative

Comments:

(continues)

153

Exhibit 4.18 *(Continued)*

Team Scorecard

Customer focus (satisfaction)		
	Current	Target

	Current	Target

	This cycle	Target

Internal process

	Current	Target

	Current	Target

Completions	Current	Target
Projects in Progress		
Reports/documents still in draft mode		

Environment/community

	Current	Target

Projects Status

XXXX
XXXX
XXXX
XXXX
XXXX
XXXX
XXXX

0% 25% 50% 75% 100%
Percentage complete

☐ Done ☐ On Track ☐ Behind ☐ Risk of Noncompletion

Learning and growth

Internal capability	Current	Target
No. of training hours provided by key staff		
Post-project reviews completed		
In-house training courses for team members		

Developing Intellectual Capital	Current	Target
Succession plans for key positions		
Staff who have verbal feedback about performance in month		

Staff satisfaction

	Current	Target

Financial

Expenditure Profile

500
400
300
200
100
0

Dec-00 Feb-01 Apr-01 Jun-01 Aug-01 Oct-01 Dec-01

◆ Planned Cumulative ■ Forecast Cumulative ✕ Actual Cumulative

Issues:

Action to be taken:

Exhibit 4.19 Team Worksheet for Completion

For each performance measure, select a team performance goal. This goal does not have to be achievable in the short term. It might represent a target for the next 6 or 12 months. In setting the goal, simply propose a target. Use any knowledge gained about better practice in your company or industry. Where a benchmark performance level can be established, use it.

For each team performance measure, answer the following:

Performance measure	Team goal	Is it accepted?	Is it a relative measure?	Is it achievable?
		☐ Yes ☐ No	☐ Yes ☐ No	☐ Yes ☐ No
		☐ Yes ☐ No	☐ Yes ☐ No	☐ Yes ☐ No
		☐ Yes ☐ No	☐ Yes ☐ No	☐ Yes ☐ No
		☐ Yes ☐ No	☐ Yes ☐ No	☐ Yes ☐ No
		☐ Yes ☐ No	☐ Yes ☐ No	☐ Yes ☐ No
		☐ Yes ☐ No	☐ Yes ☐ No	☐ Yes ☐ No

Note: Set as a relative measure (e.g., 5% better than the average for the benchmark group). This ensures a stretch target as the team will never know how well the other teams are doing until after the event. When goals are achieved, the team should "celebrate" its success and inform management, other teams, and customers.

(continues)

Exhibit 4.19 *(Continued)*

3. Displaying performance measures. Where will results be displayed each week?	
Options include:	
Team notice board	❑ Yes ❑ No
Team meeting room	❑ Yes ❑ No
Canteen/eating areas	❑ Yes ❑ No
Team intranet page	❑ Yes ❑ No
Other (company newsletter)	❑ Yes ❑ No

4. When will team/division/department/area performance measures be reviewed?

5. If there are key performance indicators (KPIs) in your area of influence, what immediate action should be taken to correct KPIs that are off target?

KPIs	Action staff should take immediately (already have delegated authority)

For business unit and organization scorecards, look at the report format section.

Exhibit 4.20   Video Road Show for Staff—Getting to Know the KPIs

Objectives:

- To ensure that all operational staff who are to operate with the KPIs are aware of who is to collect data and by when, the systems to be used, the monitoring and action to be taken by SMT, and the delegated empowerment that employees have to correct situations as they rise on a 24/7 basis

Requirements:

- Workshop administrator to help coordinate attendees
- At least three laptops, data show, screen, three electronic whiteboards, quiet workshop space away from the offices

---

9:00 A.M.	Introduction by local senior manager
9:10 A.M.	Show the video:
	• Introduction by CEO
	• The new thinking on key performance indicators presentation (*presented by a skilled presenter from the project team*):
	• The critical success factors for the organization
	• The three types of performance measures to be used
	• Selling the benefits through the "emotional drivers"
	• How the KPIs are to be collected and reported
	• Example of expected correction action that employees will be expected to take
	• The importance to the organization
	• Closing motivational statement by CEO
10:00 A.M.	**Commence workshop:** Brainstorm in groups of five to seven, from different teams. The failsafe procedures that will need to be adopted to ensure these KPIs are kept in the acceptable ranges. Also discuss the required delegated authority to ensure immediate corrective action can be taken by staff.
10:30 A.M.	Break.
10:50 A.M.	**Recommence workshop.**
11:20 A.M.	Feedback from groups and a common understanding is reached on what delegated authority has been given, and what expected actions are to take place.
12:00 noon	Conclusion and lunch.

The worksheet in Exhibit 4.21 will assist the project team to assess training needs. By this stage, the following should have been completed:

- Team performance measures
- KPI reporting frameworks
- KPI display areas

Exhibit 4.21   Assessment of Training Needs Worksheet

Supporting performance improvement—motivation		
Do training and appraisal processes need to be introduced for middle management to ensure they participate in a better practice approach to performance improvement?	❑ Yes	❑ No
Should reward options be introduced to encourage employee participation in performance improvement activities using KPIs?	❑ Yes	❑ No
If "yes," list potential options for the senior management team (SMT) to consider.		
Options	**Is the HR team supportive?**	
	❑ Yes	❑ No
	❑ Yes	❑ No
	❑ Yes	❑ No
	❑ Yes	❑ No
	❑ Yes	❑ No
	❑ Yes	❑ No
	❑ Yes	❑ No
	❑ Yes	❑ No
	❑ Yes	❑ No
	❑ Yes	❑ No
	❑ Yes	❑ No
	❑ Yes	❑ No

STEP 12 WORKSHEET: REFINING AND MODIFYING KPIs TO MAINTAIN THEIR RELEVANCE

A review mechanism must be established to ensure continual improvement. Greater understanding of performance measures leads to refinement in KPI measurement. It is important that performance improvements are logged as they develop. However, changes should be made only when the whole process is reviewed at about the 6- or 12-month mark.

It is important that KPIs are not revised in less than six months of operation to avoid a constantly changing environment (which hinders measurement). The review of CSFs and resultant modification should be done with the same level of consultation as the original development process.

The worksheet in Exhibit 4.22 should be completed by the project team to ensure that all KPIs remain relevant.

In addition, the project team will need to hold some workshops. Exhibits 4.23 and 4.24 provide outlines of workshops.

Exhibit 4.22   Refining and Modifying KPIs to Maintain Their Relevance

		Months	
1. Selecting an appropriate review time frame:	6	12	18
• Key performance indicators (KPIs)	❏	❏	❏
• Organization-wide performance indicators (PIs)	❏	❏	❏
• Division PIs	❏	❏	❏
• Team PIs	❏	❏	❏
• Key result indicators (KRIs)	❏	❏	❏
2. Since critical success factors (CSFs) were established, what major changes have occurred in markets and the external environment within which your organization operates?			

(continues)

159

Exhibit 4.22 *(Continued)*

2. Major changes *(continued)*

3. Do any of these changes:

- Reduce the significance of current CSFs? ❑ Yes ❑ No
- Suggest the need to modify or create new CSFs? ❑ Yes ❑ No
- Require change to organization-wide KPIs as a result? ❑ Yes ❑ No
- Require new CSFs to be developed? ❑ Yes ❑ No

4. How will new CSFs be communicated to all levels of the organization?

5. For each KPI and KRI, indicate the level of change achieved in performance over the last six months:

Performance measure	Performance six months ago	Current performance

Exhibit 4.22 *(Continued)*

6. Has improvement in any team performance measures reached the maximum possible level given current circumstances?	❏ Yes ❏ No
7. If "yes," is your "customer" satisfied with the performance level now being achieved?	❏ Yes ❏ No

8. If "yes," what are the risks associated with replacing these performance measures with other, new indicators?

Current performance measure	Risks if replaced

9. If there are no serious risks, what new performance measure could be introduced?

Exhibit 4.23   One-Day Focus Group Revisiting the Performance Measures

Objectives:

- To revisit the performance measures with a key group of staff and management
- To learn from experience and enhance the value gained from using performance measures

Requirements:

- A focus group selected from 15 to 30 experienced staff covering the business units, teams, area offices, and head office, and covering the different roles from administrators to senior management team members
- Workshop administrator to help coordinate attendees
- At least three laptops, data show, screen, three electronic whiteboards, quiet workshop space away from the offices

9:00 A.M.	Introduction by CEO
9:10 A.M.	The current status of performance measurement in the organization:
	• The success stories
	• What has not worked so well
	• The lessons learned
	• The current issues
	• The new technological solutions available
10:00 A.M.	**Commence workshop 1:** Revisit the critical success factors (CSFs) of the organization.
10:30 A.M.	Break.
10:50 A.M.	**Recommence workshop 1:** Short-list the CSFs to come up with five to eight CSFs.
11:20 A.M.	**Commence workshop 2:** Redesign the KRIs for the board (this task will take a further 10- to 16-week period to finalize).
12:00 noon	Lunch.
12:45 P.M.	**Commence workshop 3:** Brainstorm some new performance measures for the organization to replace or complement the existing ones.
2:00 P.M.	Workshop ends.

Exhibit 4.24   Team Performance Measures Workshop

Each team, after a suitable time frame (no sooner than six months) should hold a two-hour workshop to revisit the measures.

Revisiting team performance measures workshop

Learning Outcome: Refine your likely performance measures

Steps	Time
1. Select a chairperson, whose role is to ensure that everyone understands the outcome, understands the instructions, and has an opportunity to contribute.	
2. Look at existing team measures in the perspectives you have been allocated and ascertain the ones that need amendment.	20 minutes
3. Working in teams, use a mind-map to brainstorm the two two perspectives you have been given looking for new measures not yet used: • Group 1 discusses team *financial and internal process measures.* • Group 2 discusses team *environment/community and customer focus measures.* • Group 3 discusses *employee satisfaction and learning and growth measures.*	1 hour
4. Each group reports back on their measures; discuss only those measures that have not been covered already.	5 minutes for each group

CHAPTER 5

Templates for Reporting Performance Measures

The reporting framework must accommodate the requirements of different levels in the organization and the reporting frequency that supports timely decision making. Set out below are some better practice formats which will help speed up this vital step.

Electronic templates can be acquired from www.waymark.co.nz (for a small fee). Readers who provide additional formats to KPIformats@waymark.co.nz that are not already on the website will be able to get a discount on this fee providing Waymark Solutions decides to use them and are given the right to publish them. See www.waymark.co.nz for details.

REPORTING KEY RESULT INDICATORS IN A "DASHBOARD" TO THE BOARD

A dashboard should be a one-page display such as the two examples in Exhibits 5.1 and 5.2. The commentary should be included on this page.

A good dashboard with the key result indicators (KRIs) going in the right direction will give confidence to the board that management knows what it is doing and the "ship" is being steered in the right direction. The board can then concentrate on what they do best,

Exhibit 5.1 Nine-Graph Dashboard Example

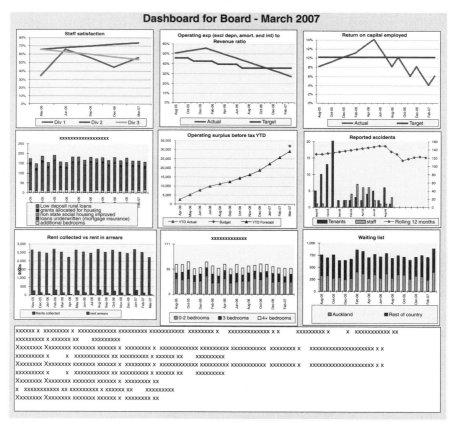

Exhibit 5.2 Six-Graph Dashboard Example

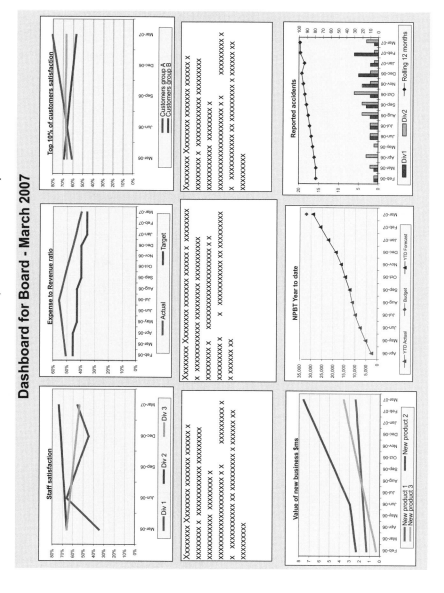

Dashboard for Board - March 2007

focusing on the horizon for icebergs in the first-class lounge instead of parking themselves on the "bridge" and thus getting in the way of the captain, who is trying to perform the important day-to-day duties. Examples of KRI board dashboard graphs can be found in Exhibit 5.3.

Exhibit 5.3 KRIs for a Board Dashboard

Customer satisfaction:

This measure needs to be measured at least every three months by using statistical samples and focusing on your top 10% to 20% of customers (the ones that are generating most if not all of your bottom line). This process does not need to be overly expensive. If you think once a year is adequate for customer satisfaction, stick to running a sports club, as you are not safe in the public or private sectors.

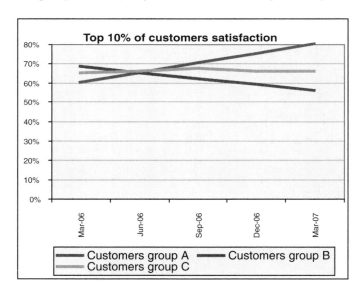

Employee satisfaction:

No different or less important than customer satisfaction. As one person said, happy staff make happy customers, who make happy owners. If you believe in this connection, run a survey now! A staff satisfaction survey need not be expensive and should never be done covering all staff; instead, it should be replaced by a rolling survey with a vertical and horizontal slice of the management and staff. (See "How to seek staff opinion and not blow your budget," *Human Resources,* June 2002, www.waymark.co.nz.)

Exhibit 5.3 *(Continued)*

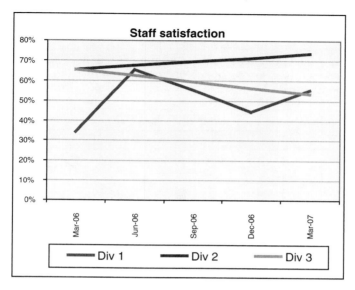

Value of new business:

All businesses in the private sector need to focus on the growth of their rising star products. It is important to monitor the pickup of this new business, especially among the top 10% to 20% of customers, who create most of the bottom line.

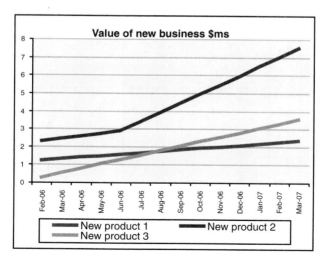

(continues)

Exhibit 5.3 *(Continued)*

Net profit before tax:

Since the board will always have a focus on the year-end, it is worthwhile to show the cumulative net profit before tax (NPBT). This graph will include the most recent forecast that should be updated on a quarterly basis bottom-up. This is the only KRI graph that starts at the beginning of the year, the rest should show a rolling 15- to 18-month trend.

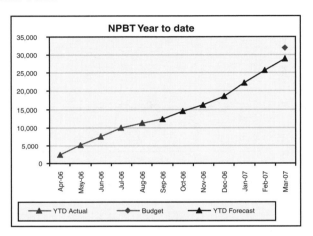

Return on capital employed:

The old stalwart of reporting. The difference now is that return on capital employed (ROCE) is no longer a key performance indicator (KPI) but a key result indicator (KRI). This graph needs to be a 12- to 15-month trend graph.

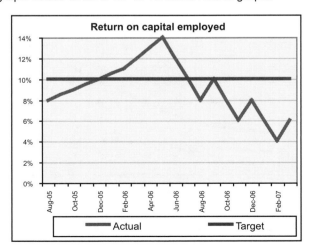

170

Exhibit 5.3 *(Continued)*

Cash flow:

This graph goes back at least 12 months and should be projected out at least six months forward.

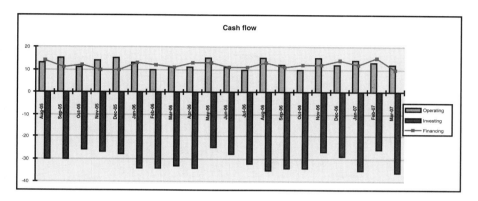

Expenses as a ratio to revenue:

The board should be interested in how effective the organization has been in utilizing technology and continuous improvement to ensure that cost of operations is tracking well against revenue.

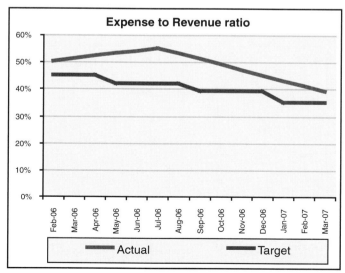

(continues)

Exhibit 5.3 *(Continued)*

Health and safety:

All boards are interested in this area, as the well-being of staff is a much higher priority these days.

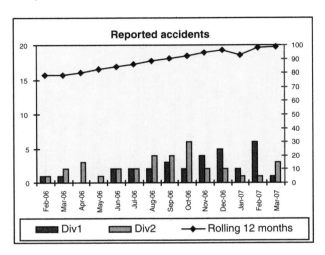

Capacity:

Monitoring the capacity of key machines and plant should go forward at least 5 to 12 months. The board needs to be aware of capacity limitations, and such a graph will help focus them on new capital expenditure requirements.

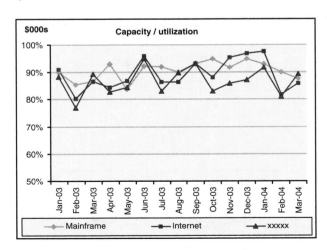

Exhibit 5.3 *(Continued)*

Operational efficiency:

A composite index based on a variety of statistics such as "delivered in full on time," portion of idle machine time (measuring key machines only).

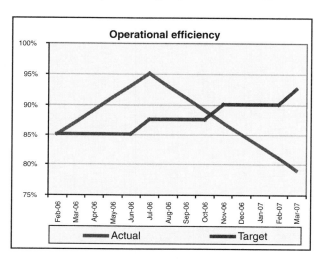

REPORTING PERFORMANCE MEASURES TO MANAGEMENT

Reporting measures to management must be timely. As mentioned throughout this book, key performance indicators (KPIs) need to be reported 24/7, daily, or at the outside weekly; other performance measures can be reported less frequently, monthly and quarterly.

Daily Reporting

The main KPIs are reported 24/7 or daily. Exhibit 5.4 shows how they should be reported on the intranet—some form of table giving the contact details, the problem, and some history so a call can be made and the manager cannot hide poor performance.

Exhibit 5.4 Intranet-Based KPI Exception Report Example

Time:

Late Planes Over 2 Hours

	Statistics of Last Stop						Contact Details			No. of Late Planes Over 1 Hour		
Flight Number	How Late	Arrival Time	Arrived Late	Left Late	Time Added	Region Manager Name	Current Time at Location	Work	Mobile	Home	Last 30 Days	30-Day Average of Last 3 Months	30-Day Average of Last 6 Months
BA1243	02:15	21:45	01:45	02:15	00:30	Pat Carruthers	18:45	xxxxx	xxxxx	xxxxx	5	4	4
BA1244	02:15	21:45	01:45	02:15	00:30	xxxxxxxxx	19:45	xxxxx	xxxxx	xxxxx	6	4	4
BA1245	02:15	21:45	01:45	02:15	00:30	xxxxxxxxx	20:45	xxxxx	xxxxx	xxxxx	7	4	4
BA1246	02:15	21:45	01:45	02:15	00:30	xxxxxxxxx	21:45	xxxxx	xxxxx	xxxxx	8	4	4
BA1247	02:15	21:45	01:45	02:15	00:30	xxxxxxxxx	22:45	xxxxx	xxxxx	xxxxx	9	4	4
BA1248	02:15	21:45	01:45	02:15	00:30	xxxxxxxxx	23:45	xxxxx	xxxxx	xxxxx	10	4	4
BA1249	02:15	21:45	01:45	02:15	00:30	xxxxxxxxx	23:45	xxxxx	xxxxx	xxxxx	11	4	4

Total: 7 planes

Another benefit of providing senior management with daily/ weekly information on the key performance areas is that the month end becomes less important. In one company where there is a 9 o'clock report every morning, management is able to have a sweepstakes on the month-end result. Talking about the monthly numbers is a small part of the meeting, which happens in the first week of the following month. In other words, if organizations report their KPIs on a 24/7 or daily basis, management knows intuitively whether the organization is having a good or bad month.

Weekly Reporting

Some KPIs only need to be reported weekly. Exhibit 5.5 is an example of how the KPIs could be presented. Note that while all the KPIs will be graphed over time, at least 15 months, only the three KPIs showing a decline in performance would be graphed. The other two KPI graphs would be maintained and used when necessary.

Monthly Reporting

There are endless ways performance measures can be shown, whether in a balanced scorecard or not. Performance measures can be shown through icons, gauges, traffic lights, and so on. Exhibit 5.6 is an example of a speedometer.

REPORTING PERFORMANCE MEASURES TO STAFF

Team Balance Scorecards

Exhibit 5.7 is an example of a team scorecard using Excel. Excel is a useful tool to design and test a template before a more robust and integrated solution is sourced.

Exhibit 5.5 Weekly KPI Report Example

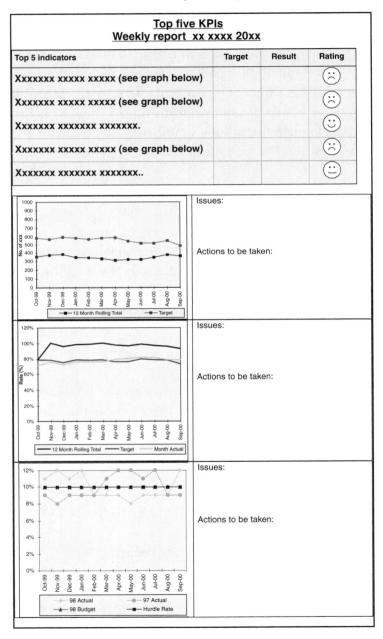

Exhibit 5.6 Speedometer Report Example

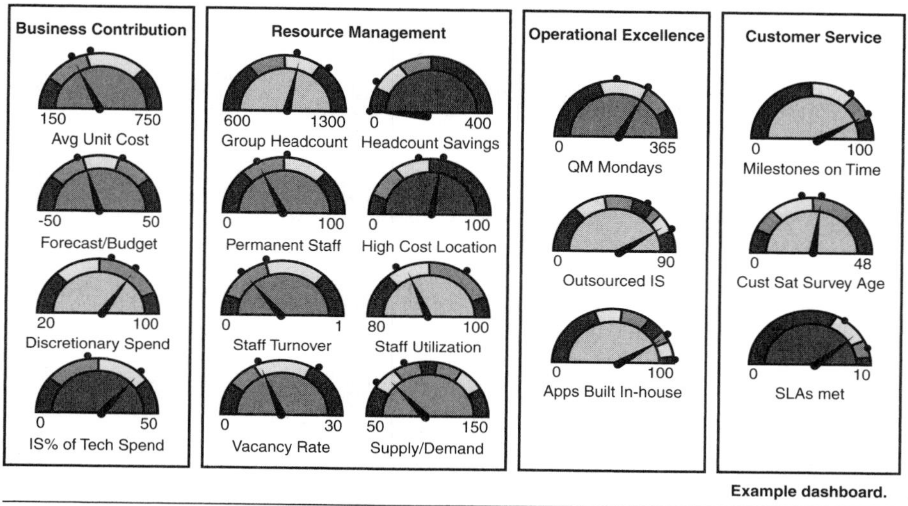

Example dashboard.

Source: www.ergometrics.com.

There are some providers who supply graphs, help you develop them, and then charge by usage such as that obtained from www. ergometrics.com.

Exhibit 5.9 provides an explanation on how the graphs in Exhibit 5.8 are interpreted.

Reporting Organizational Progress to Staff

It is a good idea to have some form of monthly icon report for staff, a report that if left on a bus would not be damaging to the organization if it found its way to a competitor. Icon reports are ideal, as they tell you what is good, what is adequate, and what needs to be improved without giving away core data. Exhibit 5.10 is an example of an icon staff report that covers the CSFs and reminds staff about the strategies.

Exhibit 5.7 Team Scorecard Designed in Excel Example

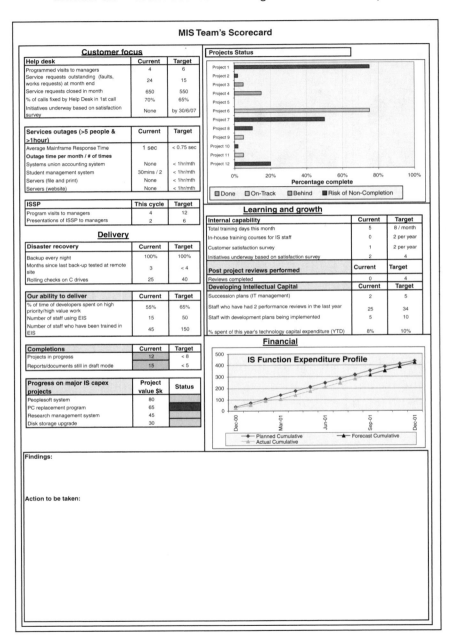

Exhibit 5.8   Team Speedometer Report

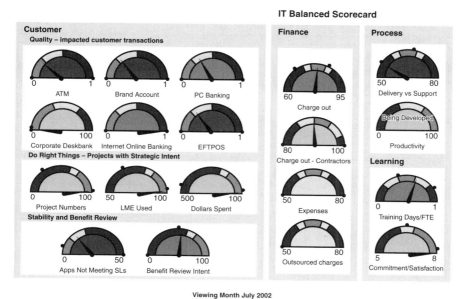

Source: www.ergometrics.com.

Exhibit 5.9   How One Company Has Made the Speedometer Give More Information

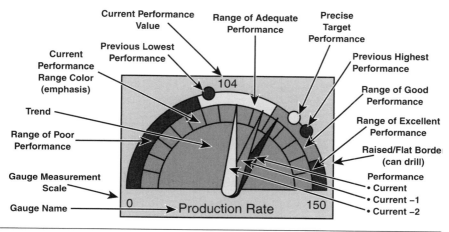

Source: www.ergometrics.com.

Exhibit 5.10   Icon Report for Staff Example

Our mission	To provide energy at the right price at the right time

Our vision for next five years	To be the preferred energy provider in the xxx

Our strategies	1. Acquiring profitable customers 2. Increase cost efficiencies 3. Innovation through our people 4. Using best business practices

Our perspectives and progress

FINANCIAL

☺ Utilization of assets

☺ Optimization of working capital, EBIT, growth, etc.

CUSTOMER FOCUS

☺ Increasing customer satisfaction

☺ Gaining profitable customers, etc.

ENVIRONMENT/ COMMUNITY

☺ Supporting local businesses

☹ Linking with future employees

☺ Community leadership, etc.

INTERNAL

☺ Delivery in full on time

☺ Optimizing technology

☹ Work accidents, etc.

EMPLOYEE SATISFACTION

☺ Positive company culture

☺ Retention of key staff

☹ Increased staff recognition, etc.

LEARNING AND GROWTH

☺ Increasing empowerment

☺ Increasing staff adaptability

☺ Coaching increasing, etc.

GRAPH FORMAT EXAMPLES

Exhibits 5.11 through 5.22 provide graphs for demonstration purposes only. The KPI team will need to be experts in graphical displays ensuring, in each case, that the graph chosen conveys the appropriate message.

Exhibit 5.11   Satisfaction Survey Response

Good features include: the use of a five-point scale, grid lines to highlight "nearly 40% of all participants were satisfied with . . . ." When showing this graph in color, you may wish to use the color red for very dissatisfied as a warning.

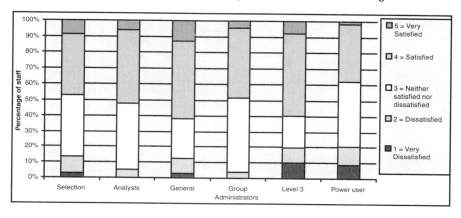

Exhibit 5.12   Satisfaction Graph Example 1

Good features include: a clear summary of a number of activities, graph incorporates an "overall" score. This graph would be shown with a yellow background.

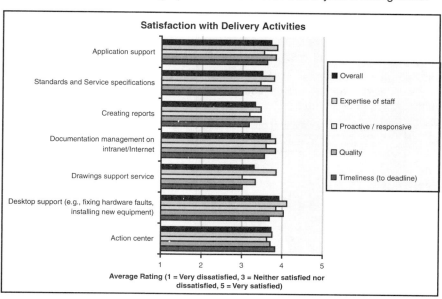

181

Exhibit 5.13   Satisfaction Graph Example 2

Good features include: this graph is particularly useful for survey responses. The vertical gridlines are lightly shaded.

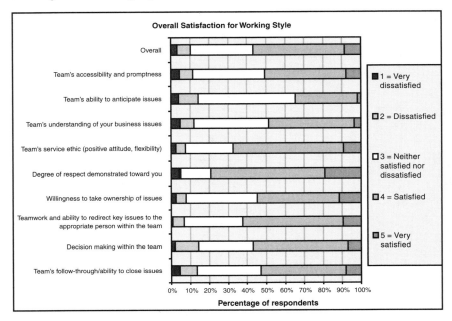

Exhibit 5.14   Scatter Diagram Example

Good features include: ease of sector comparison, overall trends clearly displayed, groups easily differentiated. Best suited for multicompany/unit comparison where similar units can be compared.

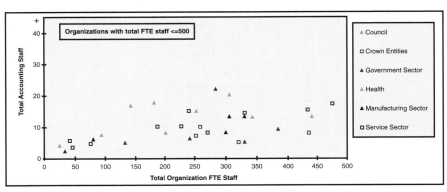

182

Exhibit 5.15 Two-Line Combination Graph Showing
Two Vertical Axes Example

Good features include: two-line combination graph comparing financial and non-financial information, and lines are shaded to match the scales. Notice that the vertical scales do not match up—there are four divisions on the left and six on the right-hand side scale. It is always best to match them up.

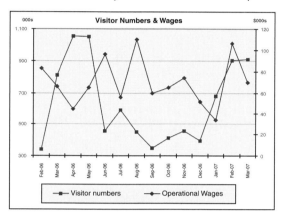

Exhibit 5.16 Line and Bar Combination Graph
Showing Two Vertical Axes Example

Good features include: a line and bar combination graph showing two performance indicators with separate vertical scales, which are colored to match the legend key. This color matching aids identification of results and comprehension. Note that grid-lines match up. Both vertical scales have same number of divisions.

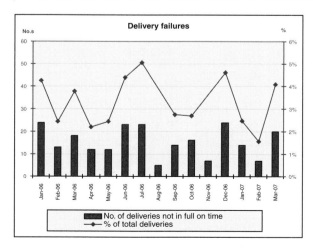

Exhibit 5.17 Stacked Bar Example

Good features include: a stacked bar graph for ease of display of both total and individual costs and not too many components. Four to five items is about the maximum.

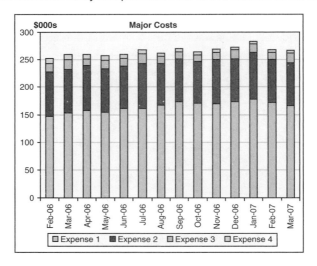

Exhibit 5.18 Horizontal Multibar Graph Example

Good features include: horizontal multibar graph allows easy comprehension and comparison.

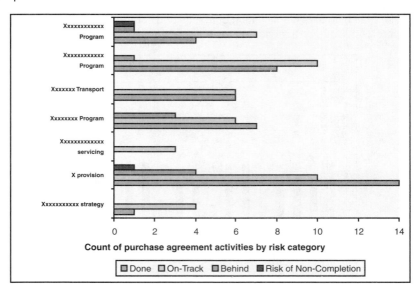

Exhibit 5.19 Multiline Graph Example

Good features include: multiline graph showing a 15-month range with three clearly
identifiable revenue streams.

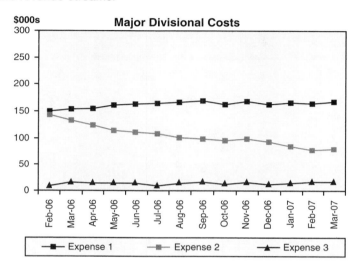

Exhibit 5.20 Acceptable Ranges Graph Example

Good features include: demonstrates acceptable range of performance as well as
indicating that improvement is being sought over time (cascading downward target).

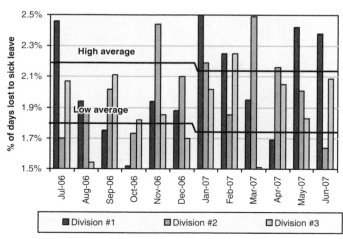

Exhibit 5.21   YTD Cumulative Example

Good features include: ready comparison between actual/forecast and budget for two significant items of expenditure covering the year in focus. Note that the budget year-to-date trend is not drawn in, as it would be a straight line in most cases, and where there is a seasonal trend the line would only be an error-prone guess.

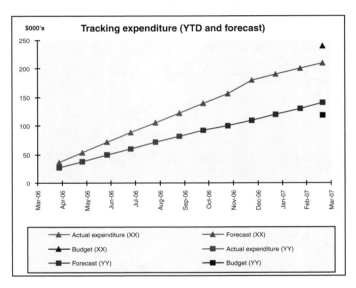

Exhibit 5.22   Actual and Forecast Comparisons Example

Good features include: three lines beginning as actual and moving on to forecast. It is a good idea to show a clear distinction between actual and forecast numbers, by changing the color of the line (e.g., from dark blue to light blue).

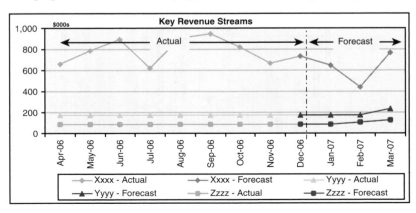

Exhibit 5.23   Better-Practice Graphics Checklist

	Tick as appropriate
1. Insert graphs into tables in a Word document to enable formatted text to be placed underneath or to the side without the need for complex tab arrangements. Graphs will also auto size to the width of the table, when pasted, saving formatting time	❑ Yes ❑ No
2. Where possible, show at least 15-month trend analysis.	❑ Yes ❑ No
3. Avoid more than three trend lines per graph, as they will probably cross over numerous times and cause confusion.	❑ Yes ❑ No
4. In line graphs, thicken the standard line to allow colors to stand out.	❑ Yes ❑ No
5. Use a pale yellow background to maximize color impact.	❑ Yes ❑ No
6. Avoid more than five divisions in a stacked bar.	❑ Yes ❑ No
7. Wherever possible, print in color.	❑ Yes ❑ No
8. Use high-quality glossy paper for the final copy.	❑ Yes ❑ No
9. Put the title of the graph in the table rather than on the graph to enable an eleventh-hour change without having to go back to the source graph.	❑ Yes ❑ No
10. Make the graph title mean something (e.g., instead of ROCE, say "ROCE is improving"; instead of EBIT, say "EBIT is declining but expected to recover.")	❑ Yes ❑ No
11. Organize workbooks so that worksheet names clearly show which graphs are in each sheet.	❑ Yes ❑ No
12. Limit graphs to four per worksheet so that they can be viewed on one screen. This also avoids searching for graphs six months later when you have forgotten which worksheet they are in.	❑ Yes ❑ No
13. Keep it simple; there are many graphical options which do not convey their message quickly (e.g., Radar, bubble, and 3D surface graphs are so difficult to read that two individuals can read the same graph and end up with very different conclusions).	❑ Yes ❑ No

(continues)

Exhibit 5.3 *(Continued)*

	Tick as appropriate
14. When paste-linking graphs into the document, select the "manual link" option as opposed to "automatic." Word attempts to update all automatic links when opening a document, and this can corrupt graphs or lock the machine if the source worksheet was not opened first.	❑ Yes ❑ No
15. Integrate graphs with the text. Do not place graphs in an appendix.	❑ Yes ❑ No
16. Experiment with several different types of graphs when displaying data for the first time.	❑ Yes ❑ No
17. When creating a graph using Excel, change the font to disable auto-sizing or the text will always dominate the graph when enlarged.	❑ Yes ❑ No

CHAPTER 6

Facilitator's Resource Kit

If you have been selected as a facilitator to assist in the development of performance measures, you will need to be completely familiar with Chapters 1 through 5 of this book. This resource kit provides you with three additional components to assist you in executing your role, namely:

1. Two introductory key performance indicator (KPI) presentations on www.bettermanagement.com. Search under Parmenter and view and listen to "Strategic Performance Management: How KPIs Show Your Organization's Health (Part I & II)." All you will need is a fast connect, sound card, speakers, and to register which is FREE. The site is an excellent source of the latest management thinking.

2. Some checklists

3. A list of typical questions (and answers) you may expect to confront in your role

REMEMBER THE FUNDAMENTALS

Coaches often talk about doing the fundamental or basic things well to ensure success. This is good advice for facilitators of KPI development, because at times the process will appear to be quite involved and complex.

As you carry out your role, always review the four foundation stones to check that your efforts are concentrated in the right areas (see Exhibit 6.1).

12 Steps and the Facilitator's Involvement in Them

It is important that the facilitator's role is one of facilitation and mentoring and not project leadership. The facilitator should have little hands-on involvement after the set-up steps have been completed.

Exhibit 6.1   Four Foundation Stones

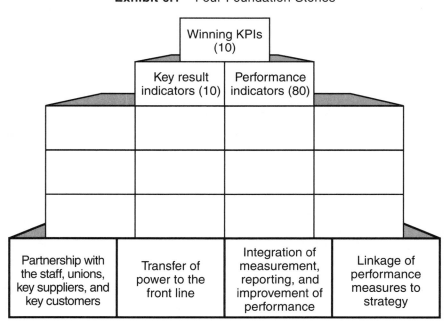

190

The manual requires the project team members, coordinators, and teams themselves to take on significant roles. The facilitator's particular role is to guide the overall process, providing assistance and resources as required.

Each of the 12 steps contains questions and or worksheets to be completed as progress is made by the project team through the implementation. The facilitator should ensure that these questions and worksheets are tailored to the organization and then followed.

A rushed and noncollaborative approach to the development and implementation of performance measures combined with a profound misunderstanding of the differences between key result indicators (KRIs), performance indicators (PIs), and KPIs will result in failure.

Checklist of the Facilitator Role

While your involvement will vary from assignment to assignment, the checklist in Exhibit 6.2 provides a draft checklist of the main tasks you will need to consider. It is important that the facilitator's role is just that and never becomes the project manager's role.

KPI Typical Questions and Answers

Introduction to the Question-and-Answer Format   Obviously, the process of KPI development will generate concerns and questions that reflect the situation and culture of the particular organization. The questions that follow represent the typical or likely issues you may need to respond to as a facilitator. The questions are divided into three broad categories:

1. Questions about why performance measures are being introduced

2. Questions about how performance measures will be introduced

3. Questions about how performance measures will be used

Exhibit 6.2   Facilitator's Role Checklist

The facilitator's role is to:	Task completed
1. Help the senior management team (SMT) pick a key performance indicator (KPI) project team.	❏ Yes ❏ No
2. Convince management that these staff need to be committed **full time.**	❏ Yes ❏ No
3. Help select a liaison person for all business units/service teams.	❏ Yes ❏ No
4. Ensure that SMT members are not on the project team.	❏ Yes ❏ No
5. Help "sell" the concept to the SMT.	❏ Yes ❏ No
6. Access performance measures and reporting templates that have been used in other organization's to avoid "reinventing the wheel."	❏ Yes ❏ No
7. Introduce case study material.	❏ Yes ❏ No
8. Obtain a sufficient level of commitment from the SMT.	❏ Yes ❏ No
9. Sell the concept to any new SMT members.	❏ Yes ❏ No
10. Guide the SMT to accept the balance scorecard perspectives recommended in this book.	❏ Yes ❏ No
11. Ensure that the KPI project team and SMT refine the hundreds of performance measures to fit the 10/80/10 rule.	❏ Yes ❏ No
12. Help the team differentiate between *key result indicators, performance indicators,* and *KPIs.*	❏ Yes ❏ No
13. Ensure that the organization does not consolidate business unit performance indicators and end up having them called KPIs.	❏ Yes ❏ No
14. The facilitator and SMT need to ensure that the project team are encouraged, given regular feedback, given recognition when milestones have been achieved, and so forth.	❏ Yes ❏ No
15. Empower and educate the KPI project team so they do not have to rely on experts to run the project.	❏ Yes ❏ No

Exhibit 6.2 *(Continued)*

The facilitator's role is to:	Task completed
16. Promote the use of existing in-house applications for database and reporting purposes during the first 12 months.	❑ Yes ❑ No
17. Help the KPI project team to set up a database to record all performance measures identified and communicate these through the KPI intranet home page.	❑ Yes ❑ No
18. Ensure that work on team performance measures does not divert the project team from ascertaining the organization's KPIs.	❑ Yes ❑ No
19. Ensure that the KPI team has made good use of reporting templates outlined in Chapter 5 before attempting to develop any of their own.	❑ Yes ❑ No
20. Ensure that the organization finds a suitable name for the scorecard reports (e.g., navigator instead of balanced scorecard).	❑ Yes ❑ No

The suggested responses to each question are derived from the philosophy and values that underlie the four foundation stones for KPI development and use.

Questions Related to the Purposes of Performance Measures

Why are we being asked to cooperate in the introduction of performance measures?

Your response should focus on two key issues:

1. Make it clear that the way performance measures are to be introduced and used is different from previous applications of performance measurement in the workplace. That is, performance measures have typically been instigated, collected, analyzed, and used by managers and supervisors. In contrast, this best-practice approach to KPI development and use is completely

concerned with involving employees in what gets measured, how things are measured, and what gets done as a result of the information. In short, a best-practice approach to performance measures cannot succeed without the cooperation, involvement, and empowerment of the organization's employees.

2. Be prepared to explain how performance measures fit in with the other strategies for improvement in the organization. This link could be related to a customer focus program, a quality improvement program, enterprise bargaining, and so forth. Making the link clear will remove any concerns about the timing of KPI introduction. That is, the "why now?" question.

Why does management need new measures of performance?

Your response should focus on three key issues:

1. The new performance measures are for everyone in the organization to use (i.e., not just management).

2. The purpose of performance measures is to enable everyone to focus on the key aspects of organizational performance that determine health and success. A best-practice approach to KPI development results in everyone's understanding what these aspects are for your organization.

3. New measures of performance are required to ensure we take a broad view of what determines health and success. That is, we need performance measures that help us to improve in relation to:

- Customer focus
- Financial performance
- Learning and growth
- Internal process
- Employee satisfaction
- Environment and community

Are these performance measures going to be used against us?

The purpose of KPIs, PIs, and KRIs in a best-practice approach is to empower employees to use the information to assist them to improve performance. Performance measure reporting does not create "report cards." They are more like a progressive scoreboard that enables teams to assess the current position and plan the response they want to take.

Questions about the Introduction of Performance Measures

Who will decide what gets measured?

Each team will select the performance measures that relate to their own efforts and actions. The three key criteria for teams to address when selecting their measures are:

1. The organization's critical success factors (CSFs) and how the team can affect them.
2. Ease of use of measure, and the ability of the team to take action based on the information.
3. A measure must be carefully vetted by the KPI team and senior management team (SMT) before it obtains the KPI status.

The teams will be assisted by the facilitator.

Do we all need the same performance measures?

No. Everyone should focus on the same organization-wide CSFs, but what they decide to measure will vary according to the team's function and how the team believes they impact on the CSFs.

Over time, as we build an integrated system of KPIs, PIs, and KRIs, your team will be able to look at a hierarchy of performance measures, as shown in Exhibit 6.3.

Can we be forced to measure a particular aspect of performance?

Forcing a team to measure something contradicts the principles of partnership and empowerment. In short, teams should be encouraged

Exhibit 6.3   Interrelated Levels of Performance
Measures in an Organization

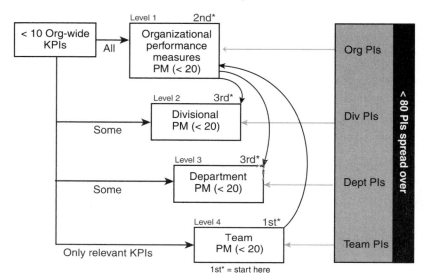

to select performance measures that relate to the organization-wide
CSFs. If it is the view of the consultative committee or equivalent
that a particular team is not measuring performance in a key area
(e.g., an aspect of customer service), they may suggest that the team
reviews its performance measures.

How many performance measures do we need?

There is no perfect number of performance measures. What you need
to consider is:

- Have we introduced performance measures that cover all the
  CSFs?
- Can we easily sustain the number of performance measures we
  are proposing to use?
- Is each particular performance measure in fact providing useful
  information that the team can use to analyze and improve the
  key processes for which they are responsible?

Often, these criteria result in up to 25 performance measures for a team. Remember that teams can modify their performance measures whenever they believe they are not meeting their needs. The 10/80/10 rule is a good guide (see Exhibit 6.4).

Do we need to start from scratch and develop totally new performance measures?

Probably not. Your goal is to develop a set of performance measures that address the CSFs for the organization. You may well be able to use some existing measures. In other cases, new performance measures may be required.

What do you do when it is difficult to measure something?

In simple terms, the best you can. Sometimes it is necessary to develop a performance measure that is a proxy for what you are seeking to track. For example, a team may want to measure morale. This can be achieved by using a survey approach. However, surveys are generally done on a sample basis and no more frequently than quarterly. The team may decide to focus on measures that are proxies for morale, such as attendance, occupational health and safety indices, or the number of errors or mistakes.

Questions Related to the Use of Performance Measures

Who decides how performance measures are used?

Under the principle of partnership, the uses and application of performance measures should be agreed to by the consultative committee (or equivalent) and each individual team.

The use of performance measures can evolve over time; however, the direction of this evolution is a subject for consultation and agreement.

Will performance measures evaluate individual performance?

No. The focus of performance measures is on key processes and key outcomes that determine organizational health and success. At the

Exhibit 6.4 10/80/10 Rule for Performance Measures

Key result indicator (10)	Tells you how you have done in a perspective
Performance indicator (80)	Tells you what to do
Key performance indicator (10)	Tells you what to do to increase performance dramatically

team level, performance measures should target team performance rather than individual performance.

Will performance measures be used for disciplinary purposes?

No, performance measures should be used to help teams to analyze and improve processes. In the case of a performance problem in relation to a team or an individual, the standard process for addressing such an issue should be pursued.

What happens if KPI target or goal is not achieved?

If a team has set some goals for improvement related to their performance measures, it is, of course, possible that these targets or goals may not be achieved.

This is not a crisis. The focus should be on analyzing why the goal could not be achieved. Through this problem-solving focus, the team can progressively identify and eliminate the barriers to the achievement of their goal.

Running Workshops

Running good workshops is an acquired skill, and the KPI team should receive specific training. If the facilitator is required to run a workshop, Exhibit 6.5 provides a preparation checklist.

Exhibit 6.5 Preparation Checklist

	Site 1	Site 2
Tasks to do before sending material		
Footer and page number on slides		
Workshop instructions prepared		
Workshop exercise sheets prepared		
Confirmed data show at site		
Confirmed white board at site		
Sent seating plan		
Week prior to workshop		
Handouts sent and have been received		
All presentations on laptop		
Tested preparations loading on to laptop		
Presentation and handout copies on USB stick		
Website loaded with reference material, if necessary		
Day before travel		
Pack hotel booking details		
Pack spare shirt and tie		
Pack gym gear and swimming trunks		
Pack clothing and toiletries as well as presentation		
Pack mouse for laptop		
Pack power cable for laptop		
Pack phone charger in brief case		

Exhibit 6.5 *(Continued)*

Day before travel *(continued)*	Site 1	Site 2
Pack spare data show cable		
Pack workshop handout master		
Pack laptop		
Pack electronic flight tickets in note-taking folder		
Pack note-taking folder in briefcase		
Pack background material in briefcase (reading on plane)		
Pack business cards		

APPENDIX

Performance Measures Database*

The key performance indicator (KPI) team will have gathered and recorded performance measures from information gained from discussions held with senior management, revisiting company archives, reviewing monthly reports, and external research. In addition, teams will, during brainstorming sessions, come up with performance measures they wish to use.

These performance measures identified need to be recorded, collated, and modified in a database that is available to all staff. This database will have a read-only facility to all employees. Amendment is permitted only by team coordinators (restricted to their area) and the KPI team (unlimited restriction).

The following table is a listing of performance measures to help start this process off. It will be a valuable resource when looking at performance measures during brainstorming sessions. You can acquire this table electronically from www.waymark.co.nz (for a small fee). Readers who contribute additional measures to KPImeasures@

---

*This material is extracted from the Waymark Database of Performance Measures.

waymark.co.nz will be rewarded with a discount on this fee. See www.waymark.co.nz for details.

It is advisable not to provide attendees with this list until they have performed some brainstorming and come up with measures themselves. To introduce this list too early will lead to a narrowing of the potential performance measures.

Some of the performance indicators (PIs) in this list may well be KPIs, others will be KRIs. It is up to the KPI project team to ascertain which of the three categories the final set of performance measures should be.

Note that the recommended category headings for a performance measures database are:

- Description of the performance measure

- Explanation as to how the performance measure is calculated

- The type of performance measure (KRI, PI, KPI)

- Person responsible for obtaining measurement

- System where data is sourced from or how it is to be gathered

- Refinements that may be required to produce "real time" information

- Which balanced scorecard perspective(s) the performance measure impacts

- Recommended display (type of graph, etc.)

- How often it should be measured

- Linkage of measure to the CSFs

- The required delegated authority that staff will need to have in order to take immediate remedial action

- The teams who have chosen to measure it (this can act like a selection list). You may have a column for each team with a "yes" or "✓" indicating selection.

Name of Measure	Frequency of Measure	BSC Perspective	Applicable BSC Teams	Applicable Sectors	Strategic Objective
Dollar revenue gained from top customers in the week	Weekly	Customer satisfaction	Sales and Marketing	All private sector	Increase profitability
Percentage of customers with key attributes (ones that generate most profit)	Quarterly	Customer satisfaction	Sales and Marketing	All private sector	Increase profitability
Percentage of successful/unsuccessful tenders	Quarterly	Customer satisfaction	Sales and Marketing	All private sector	Increase profitability
Actual delivery date versus promised date	Weekly	Customer satisfaction	Production	All private sector	Efficient operations
Average customer size by category (category A being the top 20% of customers)	Monthly	Customer satisfaction	Sales and Marketing	All private sector	Increase profitability
Average time from customer enquiry to sales team response	Weekly	Customer satisfaction	Sales and Marketing	All private sector	Efficient operations
Average time to resolve complaints, to get credits for product quality problems, etc.	Weekly	Customer satisfaction	Sales	All private sector	Retention of customers/minimize negative comment in the marketplace
Number of stock outs	Weekly	Customer satisfaction	Production	All private sector	Efficient operations
Brand image index (%) based from market research	Monthly	Customer satisfaction	Sales and Marketing	All private sector	Increase profitability
Cost of quality correction—rework, rejects, warrantees, returns and allowances, inspection labor, and equipment, complaint processing costs	Weekly	Customer satisfaction	Quality assurance (QA) team	All private sector	Efficient operations
Customer acquisition (rate business unit attracts or wins new customers or business)	Monthly	Customer satisfaction	Sales and Marketing	All private sector	Increase profitability

(continues)

Name of Measure	Frequency of Measure	BSC Perspective	Applicable BSC Teams	Applicable Sectors	Strategic Objective
Customer loyalty index (percentage of customer retention within customer categories)	Quarterly	Customer satisfaction	Sales and Marketing	All private sector	Long-term relationship with profitable customers
Number of customer service initial inquiries to follow-up	Weekly	Customer satisfaction	Sales and Marketing	All private sector	Increasing sales
Customers lost (number or percentage)	Weekly/Monthly	Customer satisfaction	Sales and Marketing	All private sector	Increase profitability
Number of defect goods on installation (dead on arrival, including those that occur within the first 90 days of operation)	Weekly	Customer satisfaction	Sales and Marketing, QA team	All private sector	More reliable products
Sales of goods and services taken up by key customers—top 10% to 20% of customers	Monthly	Customer satisfaction	Sales and Marketing	All private sector	Increase profitability
Direct communications to key customers in month (average number of contacts made with the key customers)	Monthly	Customer satisfaction	Sales and Marketing	All private sector	Increase profitability
Market share (proportion of business in a given market)	Quarterly	Customer satisfaction	Sales and Marketing	All private sector	Increase profitability
Number of customer referrals	Monthly	Customer satisfaction	Sales and Marketing	All private sector	Increase profitability
Number of incidents where senior management needed to instigate the remedial action	Monthly	Customer satisfaction	Sales and Marketing	All private sector	Efficient operations
Number of proactive visits to top 10% of customers	Monthly	Customer satisfaction	Sales and Marketing	All private sector	Increase profitability
Number of client relationships producing significant net profit (over $X million)	Quarterly	Customer satisfaction	Sales	All private sector	Increase profitability

Measure	Frequency		Responsible party	Sector	Objective
Number of contacts with customer during project and post-project wrap-up (major projects only)	Monthly	Customer satisfaction	Project teams	All private sector	Increase profitability
Number of credits/returns from key customers	Weekly	Customer satisfaction	Accounting	All private sector	Increase profitability
Number of visits made to core customers in a week	Monthly	Customer satisfaction	Sales and Marketing	All private sector	Long-term relationship with profitable customers
Order entry error rate	Weekly	Customer satisfaction	Sales and back office teams entering orders	All private sector	Efficient operations
Order frequency (number of orders coming in per day/week)	Weekly	Customer satisfaction	Sales and Marketing	All private sector	Efficient operations
Orders canceled by reason (up to five categories)	Weekly	Customer satisfaction	Sales	All private sector	Long-term relationship with profitable customers
Quality problems detected during product audits in the field	When audits performed	Customer satisfaction	Sales and Marketing, QA team	All private sector	Long-term relationship with profitable customers
Customer satisfaction of top 10% of customers	Quarterly	Customer satisfaction	Sales and Marketing	All private sector	Increase profitability
Sales closed as a percentage of total sales proposals	Monthly	Customer satisfaction	Sales and Marketing	All private sector	Increase profitability
Service expense per customer category	Periodically	Customer satisfaction	Sales and Marketing	All private sector	Efficient operations
Time elapsed since repeat business with category A customers (top 20% or top 10% customers)	Weekly	Customer satisfaction	Sales and Marketing	All private sector	Increase profitability
Abandon rate—caller gives up	Weekly	Customer satisfaction	Information technology (IT) communications	All sectors	Minimize negative comment in the marketplace

(continues)

205

Name of Measure	Frequency of Measure	BSC Perspective	Applicable BSC Teams	Applicable Sectors	Strategic Objective
Calls answered first time (not having to be transferred to another party)	Daily and in some cases 24/7	Customer satisfaction	IT help desk, call centers	All sectors	Efficient operations
Calls on hold longer than xx seconds	Daily and in some cases 24/7	Customer satisfaction	IT commu- nications	All sectors	Minimizing negative comment in the marketplace
Complaints not resolved in two hours	Daily	Customer satisfaction	Sales and Marketing	All sectors	Retention of customers/minimizing negative comment in the marketplace
Complaints not resolved on first call	Daily	Customer satisfaction	Sales and Marketing	All sectors	Retention of customers/minimizing negative comment in the marketplace
Credit request processing time	Weekly	Customer satisfaction	Accounting	All sectors	Retention of customers/minimizing negative comment in the marketplace
Key customer satisfaction	Three to four times a year and in some cases continuously	Customer satisfaction	Sales and Marketing, service delivery teams	All sectors	Retention of customers/increase sales
In-house customer satisfaction percentage	Two times a year	Customer satisfaction	All teams	All sectors	Improve employee satisfaction and productivity

Measure	Frequency	Perspective	Team	Sector	Strategic objective
Late projects by manager (a list for internal projects and a list for client projects)	Weekly	Customer satisfaction	Project teams	All sectors	Efficient operations
Number of variations to contract by type	Monthly	Customer satisfaction	Sales and Marketing	All sectors	Efficient operations
Number of Quality Service Guarantees issued (refund for poor service)	Weekly/monthly	Customer satisfaction	QA team	All sectors	Increase profitability
Number of outstanding retention installments (monitoring close-out)	Monthly	Customer satisfaction	Sales and Accounting team	All sectors where customers retain a sum of money until satisfactory completion	Increase profitability
Orders shipped, which are complete and on time (delivery in full on time)	Daily and in some cases 24/7	Customer satisfaction	Production control, dispatch, etc.	All sectors who dispatch goods	Efficient operations
The mean time between QA failures	Daily	Customer satisfaction	Production	Manufacturing	Efficient operations
Actual client projects on time (percent of total) and cost versus budget (percent of budget)	Monthly	Customer satisfaction	Project teams	Service	Retention of customers/minimizing negative comment in the marketplace
Time people waited in line	Daily	Customer satisfaction	Sales	Service	Retention of customers/minimizing negative comment in the marketplace
Service requests outstanding (faults, works requests) at month end	Quarterly	Customer satisfaction	Service teams	Service	Retention of customers/minimizing negative comment in the marketplace

(continues)

Name of Measure	Frequency of Measure	BSC Perspective	Applicable BSC Teams	Applicable Sectors	Strategic Objective
Surrender ratio of equipment or service (where service or equipment is on a monthly contract)	Monthly	Customer satisfaction	Sales and Marketing	Service	Long-term relationship with profitable customers
Number of applicants for employment at the company	Quarterly	Employee (Other)	Human Resources (HR)	All sectors	Desirable place to work
Percentage of staff working flexible hours	Monthly	Employee satisfaction	HR	All sectors	Happy employees, make happy customers, which make happy shareholders
Analysis of absenteeism	Monthly	Employee satisfaction	HR, all teams	All sectors	Happy employees, make happy customers, which make happy shareholders
Employee complaint resolution timelines and effectiveness	Monthly	Employee satisfaction	HR	All sectors	Happy employees make happy customers, which make happy shareholders
Employee satisfaction per survey	Every employee survey (three to four times a year)	Employee satisfaction	All teams	All sectors	Happy employees make happy customers, which make happy shareholders
Number of employees who have received recognition in last week, two weeks, month	Weekly	Employee satisfaction	HR	All sectors	Happy employees make happy customers, which make happy shareholders
Empowerment index, number of staff and managers who say they are empowered (from staff survey)	Every employee survey (three to four times a year)	Employee satisfaction	HR	All sectors	Happy employees make happy customers, which make happy shareholders

Measure	Frequency	Category	Owner	Scope	Rationale
Length of service of staff who have left	Monthly	Employee satisfaction	HR	All sectors	Happy employees make happy customers, which make happy shareholders
Number of days working overseas on jobs	Quarterly	Employee satisfaction	HR	All sectors	Happy employees make happy customers, which make happy shareholders
Number of recognition events and awards to staff planned for next four weeks, next eight weeks	Weekly	Employee satisfaction	HR	All sectors	Happy employees make happy customers, which make happy shareholders
Number of potential recruits that come from employee referrals	Quarterly	Employee satisfaction	HR	All sectors	Happy employees make happy customers, which make happy shareholders
Recruitment rating (survey on all new employees)	Every employee survey (three to four times a year)	Employee satisfaction	HR	All sectors	Happy employees make happy customers, which make happy shareholders
Satisfaction with a balanced working and nonworking life (from staff survey)	Every employee survey (three to four times a year)	Employee satisfaction	HR	All sectors	Efficient operations
Attendance numbers for social club functions	Quarterly	Employee satisfaction	HR	All sectors	Happy employees make happy customers, which make happy shareholders
Staff turnover by type (resignations, end of contract, temporary staff, terminations)	Monthly	Employee satisfaction	HR, all teams	All sectors	Happy employees make happy customers, which make happy shareholders

(continues)

Name of Measure	Frequency of Measure	BSC Perspective	Applicable BSC Teams	Applicable Sectors	Strategic Objective
Community/environmental satisfaction index from external survey	Periodic survey of local community's perception of company	Environment	Public Relations	All sectors	Working well with the community and environment
Volunteer retention/recruitment	Monthly	Environment	Operations	Charity	Efficient operations
Emissions from production into the environment (number)	Weekly	Environment	Production	Manufacturing	Reducing environmental impact
Energy consumed per unit, BTU/sales	Weekly	Environment	Production	Manufacturing	Reducing environmental impact
Percentage of recycled material used as raw material input	Weekly	Environment	Production	Manufacturing	Reducing environmental impact
Percentage of waste generated/recycled	Weekly	Environment	Production	Manufacturing	Reducing environmental impact
Waste and scrap produced	Weekly	Environment	Production	Manufacturing	Reducing environmental impact
Water consumption and/or discharge per production unit (or by per employee, or per sales dollar)	Weekly	Environment	Production	Manufacturing	Reducing environmental impact
Number of employees involved in community activities	Quarterly	Environment/ Community	HR	All sectors	Working well with the community and environment
Dollars donated to the community	Quarterly	Environment/ Community	Public Relations (PR)	All sectors	Positive public perception
Percentage of local residents in total workforce	Quarterly	Environment/ Community	PR	All sectors	Positive public perception

Measure	Frequency	Category	Department	Sector	Objective
Entries to environment/community awards to be completed in next three months	Monthly	Environment/Community	Operations	All sectors	Positive public perception
Number of environmental complaints received in a week	Weekly	Environment/Community	PR	All sectors	Positive public perception
Number of external charity volunteers trained by company staff	Quarterly	Environment	Operations	Charity	Working well with the community and environment
Number of firms employees involved in up-skilling local community organizations	Quarterly	Environment/Community	PR	All sectors	Positive public perception
Number of media coverage events	Monthly	Environment/Community	PR	All sectors	Positive public perception
Number of photos in paper	Monthly	Environment/Community	PR	All sectors	Positive public perception
Number of sponsorship projects undertaken by company	Quarterly	Environment/Community	PR	All sectors	Positive public perception
Number of students recruited for holiday work	Quarterly	Environment/Community	PR	All sectors	Positive public perception
Percentage of current projects that are environmentally friendly	Monthly	Environment/Community	PR	Construction	Reducing environmental impact
Percentage complete to percentage billed by job	Monthly	Financial	Operations	All private sector	Increase profitability
Percentage of category A customers covered by partnership projects	Quarterly	Financial	Sales and Marketing	All private sector	Increase profitability
Percentage of customers paying cash up front on commencement of project	Monthly	Financial	Accounting	All private sector	Increase profitability
Percentage of profitability per major project	Quarterly	Financial	Accounting	All private sector	Increase profitability

(continues)

211

Name of Measure	Frequency of Measure	BSC Perspective	Applicable BSC Teams	Applicable Sectors	Strategic Objective
Percentage of sales that have arisen from cross-selling among business units	Monthly	Financial	Sales and Marketing	All private sector	Efficient operations
Percentage of successful tenders	Monthly	Financial	Sales and Marketing	All private sector	Increase profitability
Percentage of top ten customers' business	Quarterly	Financial	Sales and Marketing	All private sector	Increase profitability
Accounts receivable turnover	Monthly	Financial	Accounting	All private sector	Efficient operations
Average number of days spent as stock in hand	Monthly	Financial	Stock control	All private sector	Increase profitability
Bad debt percentage to turnover	Monthly	Financial	Accounting	All private sector	Increase profitability
Cash flow ($)	Monthly	Financial	Accounting	All private sector	Increase profitability
Cash-to-cash cycle—length of time from cash out to cash in	Monthly	Financial	Accounting	All private sector	Increase profitability
Contribution to revenue, or contribution margin (%)	Monthly	Financial	Accounting	All private sector	Increase profitability
Customer and product-line profitability	Quarterly	Financial	Sales and Marketing	All private sector	Efficient operations
Days in accounts payable	Quarterly	Financial	Accounting	All private sector	Maintaining supplier relationships
Days in inventory	Monthly	Financial	Accounting	All private sector	Increase profitability
Days sales in receivables	Monthly	Financial	Accounting	All private sector	Efficient operations

Dealer profitability	Monthly	Financial	Sales and Marketing	All private sector	Increase profitability
Dealer satisfaction survey	Monthly	Financial	Sales and Marketing	All private sector	Efficient operations
Economic value added per employee ($)	Monthly	Financial	Accounting	All private sector	Increase profitability
Gross margin by business	Monthly	Financial	Accounting	All private sector	Increase profitability
Indirect expenses as a percentage of sales	Monthly	Financial	Accounting	All private sector	Efficient operations
Marketing expense per customer ($)	Quarterly	Financial	Marketing	All private sector	Efficient operations
Net income by business	Monthly	Financial	Accounting	All private sector	Increase profitability
New business—by occurrence type (e.g., referrals, promotional drive, prospecting, website, etc.)	Monthly	Financial	Sales and Marketing	All private sector	Increase profitability
Number of profitable customers	Quarterly	Financial	Sales and Marketing	All private sector	Increase profitability
Number of projects with all progress payments paid	Quarterly	Financial	Accounting	All private sector	Efficient operations
Number of winning tenders that have created losses	Monthly	Financial	Operations	All private sector	Increase profitability
Percentage revenues from new products or service	Quarterly	Financial	Sales and Marketing	All private sector	Increase sales
Profits from new products or business operations ($)	Monthly	Financial	Sales and Marketing	All private sector	Increase profitability
Profits/employee ($)	Monthly	Financial	Accounting	All private sector	Increase profitability

(continues)

213

Name of Measure	Frequency of Measure	BSC Perspective	Applicable BSC Teams	Applicable Sectors	Strategic Objective
Return on capital employed	Monthly	Financial	Accounting	All private sector	Efficient operations
Return on net asset value	Monthly	Financial	Accounting	All private sector	Efficient operations
Return on equity	Monthly	Financial	Accounting	All private sector	Increase profitability
Revenues/employee ($)	Monthly	Financial	Accounting	All private sector	Increase profitability
Revenues/total assets (%)	Monthly	Financial	Accounting	All private sector	Increase profitability
Sales by manager	Monthly	Financial	Sales and Marketing	All private sector	Increase profitability
Sales growth rate by market segment	Quarterly	Financial	Sales and Marketing	All private sector	Increase profitability
Credit rating	Monthly	Financial	Accounting	All sectors	Increase profitability
Debt-to-equity ratio	Monthly	Financial	Accounting	All sectors	Increase profitability
Investment in development of new markets ($)	Quarterly	Financial	Sales	All sectors	Innovation
IT expense as a percentage of total administrative expense	Quarterly	Financial	IT, Accounting, or Finance	All sectors	Efficient operations
People/headquarters costs	Monthly	Financial	Accounting	All sectors	Efficient operations
Percentage unprofitable customers	Monthly	Financial	Sales and Marketing	All sectors	Increase profitability
Progress on major IS CAPEX projects	Monthly	Financial	IT, Accounting, or Finance	All sectors	Efficient operations

214

Measure	Frequency	Perspective	Function	Sector	Objective
Teams expenditure profile for year to date (tracks actual and expected against planned expenditure profile for year)	Monthly	Financial	IT	All sectors	Efficient operations
Total assets/employee ($)	Monthly	Financial	Accounting	All sectors	Increase profitability
Value of work in progress ($)	Monthly	Financial	Operations	All sectors	Efficient operations
Average cost of maintaining a customer account ($)	Quarterly	Financial	Operations	Banking	Increase profitability
Value of mortgage offers ($)	Monthly	Financial	Operations	Banking	Increase profitability
Value of personal loan advances ($)	Monthly	Financial	Operations	Banking	Increase profitability
Administrative expense as a percentage of gross premium	Quarterly	Financial	Accounting	Insurance	Increase profitability
Percentage chargeable work/nonrecoverable	Weekly	Financial	All service teams	Service	Increase profitability
Budgeted time against actual time on weekly basis	Weekly	Financial	Accounting	Service	Increase profitability
Percentage of brand dominance in market	Quarterly	Internal process	Sales and Marketing	All private sector	Increase profitability
Percentage of invoices processed within the week	Monthly	Internal Process	Operations	All private sector	Efficient operations
Accuracy and completeness of specifications for orders	Weekly	Internal process	Sales	All private sector	Efficient operations
Average age of company patents (number)	Quarterly	Internal Process	Research and development (R&D)	All private sector	Innovation
Changes to orders after initial placement—controllable and uncontrollable	Weekly	Internal process	Sales	All private sector	Efficient operations
Excess inventory—anything above normal requirements	Monthly	Internal process	Production	All private sector	Increase profitability

(continues)

Name of Measure	Frequency of Measure	BSC Perspective	Applicable BSC Teams	Applicable Sectors	Strategic Objective
Inventory items above/below target limits	Monthly	Internal process	Production	All private sector	Efficient operations
Manufacturing cycle effectiveness = processing/ throughput time	Weekly	Internal process	Operations	All private sector	Increase profitability
Manufacturing process quality measures re-work (how many items make it through the process without being reworked at any stage) %	Weekly	Internal process	Operations	All private sector	Increase profitability
Merchandise availability measure of inventory turns on selected key items	Monthly	Internal process	Operations	All private sector	Increase profitability
Number of improvements made to existing products	Monthly	Internal process	R&D	All private sector	Innovation
Number of profitable new products (over $XX and greater than X% gross margin)	Quarterly	Internal process	R&D	All private sector	Increase profitability
Outage hours per month	Monthly	Internal process	Production	All private sector	Efficient operations
Patents filed and issued that have been incorporated into products	Monthly	Internal process	R&D	All private sector	Efficient operations
Percentage of products for which the first design of a device fully met the customer's functional specification	Monthly	Internal process	Production	All private sector	Efficient operations
Potential revenue in sales pipeline	Weekly	Internal process	Sales and Marketing	All private sector	Increase profitability
Pricing accuracy	Weekly	Internal process	Sales	All private sector	Efficient operations
Product-development cycle time of major new projects	Quarterly	Internal process	R&D	All private sector	Increase profitability

Measure	Frequency	Perspective	Department	Sector	Objective
Production amount that passes to next stage in production	Weekly	Internal process	Operations	All private sector	Increase profitability
Production cycle time (time in each stage)	Monthly	Internal process	Operations	All private sector	Increase profitability
Quality problems due to equipment failure	Monthly	Internal process	Production	All private sector	Efficient operations
Queue production time ratio	Monthly	Internal process	Production	All private sector	Efficient operations
Ratio of new products (less than X years old) to full company catalog (%)	Quarterly	Internal process	Operations	All private sector	Innovation
R&D percentage of sales from propriety products	Quarterly	Internal process	R&D	All private sector	Increase profitability
Research and Development time to develop next generation of products	Quarterly	Internal process	R&D	All private sector	Increase profitability
Sales to selling costs ratio	Monthly	Internal process	Sales and Marketing	All private sector	Increase profitability
Timeliness and accuracy of price quotations and requests for samples	Weekly	Internal process	Sales	All private sector	Efficient operations
Dollars saved by employee suggestions	Quarterly	Internal process	Accounting	All sectors	Efficient operations
Percentage completed timesheets by deadline	Monthly	Internal process	All teams	All sectors	Efficient operations
Percentage of hours spent on R&D	Quarterly	Internal process	R&D	All sectors	Innovation
Percentage of payments (nonpayroll) right amount paid made on time	Monthly	Internal process	Accounting	All sectors	Efficient operations
Percentage of payments (payroll) right amount paid made on time	Monthly	Internal process	Payroll	All sectors	Efficient operations

(continues)

Name of Measure	Frequency of Measure	BSC Perspective	Applicable BSC Teams	Applicable Sectors	Strategic Objective
Percentage of payments made by direct credit	Monthly	Internal process	Accounting	All sectors	Efficient operations
Percentage of requests for help fixed by Help Desk during the first phone call	Monthly	Internal process	IT	All sectors	Efficient operations
Percentage of sales invoices issued on time	Monthly	Internal process	Sales	All sectors	Efficient operations
Percentage of time program developers have spent on programming (tracking nonproductive time)	Monthly	Internal process	All teams, especially IT	All sectors	Efficient operations
Percentage spent of this year's technology capital expenditure	Monthly	Internal process	IT	All sectors	Efficient operations
Accidents per 100,000 hours worked	Monthly	Internal process	HR	All sectors	Efficient operations
Accounting system downtime (8 A.M. to 6 P.M.)	Monthly	Internal process	Accounting	All sectors	Efficient operations
Adherence to schedule—tasks being performed on time	Monthly	Internal process	Production	All sectors	Efficient operations
Asset utilization rates of major machines	Monthly	Internal process	Operations	All sectors	Efficient operations
Availability of Human Resources system	Monthly	Internal process	HR	All sectors	Efficient operations
Average mainframe response time	Monthly	Internal process	IT	All sectors	Efficient operations
Back-to-work programs for staff who have been absent for more than three weeks	Monthly	Internal process	HR	All sectors	Efficient operations
Backup every night this month	Weekly	Internal process	IT	All sectors	Efficient operations

Measure	Frequency	Perspective	Department	Scope	Strategic theme
Date of last backup tested at remote site	Quarterly	Internal process	IT	All sectors	Efficient operations
Billing accuracy	Monthly	Internal process	Accounting	All sectors	Efficient operations
Business development expense/administrative expense	Monthly	Internal process	Accounting	All sectors	Efficient operations
Completion of projects on time and budget (% or $ of total projects)	Monthly	Internal process	All teams	All sectors	Skilled and experienced workforce
Current users of xxx system	Monthly	Internal process	IT	All sectors	Efficient operations
Employees on self-managing teams	Quarterly	Internal process	HR	All sectors	Efficient operations
Faults or service requests closed in month	Monthly	Internal process	IT	All sectors	Efficient operations
Initiatives underway based on satisfaction survey	Monthly	Internal process	All teams	All sectors	Efficient operations
Investment in research ($)	Quarterly	Internal process	R&D	All sectors	Innovation
IT capacity	Monthly	Internal process	IT	All sectors	Efficient operations
Key work carried out by contractors	Monthly	Internal process	HR	All sectors	Efficient operations
Last update of intranet page	Monthly	Internal process	All teams	All sectors	Efficient operations
Lost time injury frequency (graph)	Weekly	Internal process	HR	All sectors	Efficient operations
Managers accessing the general ledger (time)	Monthly	Internal process	Accounting	All sectors	Efficient operations

(continues)

Name of Measure	Frequency of Measure	BSC Perspective	Applicable BSC Teams	Applicable Sectors	Strategic Objective
Manual transaction to automated electronic transaction ratio	Monthly	Internal process	All teams	All sectors	Efficient operations
Median patent age in key products	Quarterly	Internal process	R&D	All sectors	Innovation
Monthly finance report to the report to CEO	Monthly	Internal process	Accounting or Finance, HR, IT	All sectors	Efficient operations
Monthly report to budget holders	Monthly	Internal process	Accounting	All sectors	Efficient operations
Number of accounts payable invoices paid late	Monthly	Internal process	Accounting	All sectors	Efficient operations
Number of customer calls in test week (e.g., third week of month)	Monthly	Internal process	Accounting	All sectors	Efficient operations
Number of innovations introduced in last 3, 6, 9, 12 months	Quarterly	Internal process	Operations	All sectors	Innovation
Number of managers accessing the general ledger	Monthly	Internal process	Accounting	All sectors	Efficient operations
Number of strategic supply relationships	Monthly	Internal process	Procurement	All sectors	Efficient operations
Number of systems that have been integrated with other company systems	Quarterly	Internal process	IT	All sectors	Efficient operations
Number of progress payments due that have not yet been invoiced	Monthly	Internal process	Operations	All sectors	Efficient operations
Number/percentage of projects completed on time/budget	Monthly	Internal process	Operations	All sectors	Efficient operations

Measure	Frequency	Perspective	Team	Sector	Objective
Number of management team meetings last week (or number of management meetings planned for next five days)	Monthly	Internal process	All teams	All sectors	Efficient operations
Number of IT contractors as a percentage of IT employees	Quarterly	Internal process	IT, HR	All sectors	Efficient operations
Number of critical assets in a catastrophic state	Monthly	Internal process	Operations	All sectors	Efficient operations
Number of employees	Monthly	Internal process	HR	All sectors	Efficient operations
Number of post-project reviews/debriefs	Quarterly	Internal process	Operations	All sectors	Efficient operations
Number of staff trained in first aid	Quarterly	Internal process	HR	All sectors	Healthy and safe work environment
Number of times schedule slipped in month	Monthly	Internal process	All teams	All sectors	Efficient operations
Orders and reports shipped by express services	Monthly	Internal process	All teams	All sectors	Efficient operations
Number of overdue reports/documents	Weekly	Internal process	All teams	All sectors	Efficient operations
Policy and procedures sections updated this month	Monthly	Internal process	All teams	All sectors	Efficient operations
Percent of operational purchases from certified vendors	Monthly	Internal process	Operations	All sectors	Maintain supplier relationships
Percent of positive feedback from employees after attending meetings (every meeting rated via intranet)	Monthly	Internal process	All teams	All sectors	Efficient operations
Product changes to correct design deficiencies	Quarterly	Internal process	Design	All sectors	Efficient operations

(continues)

221

Name of Measure	Frequency of Measure	BSC Perspective	Applicable BSC Teams	Applicable Sectors	Strategic Objective
R&D as a percentage of sales	Quarterly	Internal process	Research	All sectors	Innovation
R&D resources/total resources	Monthly	Internal process	IT	All sectors	Efficient operations
Resolution of queries in same day	Monthly	Internal process	All teams	All sectors	Efficient operations
Response time to inquiries and special requests	Monthly	Internal process	All teams	All sectors	Efficient operations
Safety measures—accidents, days lost by reason	Monthly	Internal process	HR, all teams	All sectors	Healthy and safe work environment
Service requests (faults, works requests) logged	Monthly	Internal process	IT	All sectors	Efficient operations
Slow-moving and obsolete inventory	Quarterly	Internal process	Production	All sectors	Increase profitability
Staff who have attended the stress management course	Monthly	Internal process	HR	All sectors	Efficient operations
Staff with > 30 days leave owing	Monthly	Internal process	HR	All sectors	Efficient operations
Stakeholder feedback (on activities, working style, and communication)	When survey performed	Internal process	PR	All sectors	Efficient operations
Number of succession plans for key positions	Quarterly	Internal process	HR	All sectors	Efficient operations
Suppliers on the accounts payable ledger	Monthly	Internal process	Accounting	All sectors	Efficient operations

Measure	Frequency	Perspective	Team	Sector	Objective
Time spent on quality improvement activities	Monthly	Internal process	All teams	All sectors	Efficient operations
Units/labor hour and labor dollar for direct, indirect, and total labor costs	Monthly	Internal process	Production	All sectors	Efficient operations
Visits to managers planned next week	Monthly	Internal process	All teams	All sectors	Efficient operations
Conversion rate of home-buying certificates to mortgage offers	Monthly	Internal process	Branches	Banking	Efficient operations
Value of retail investment receipts (gross) dollars	Monthly	Internal process	Accounting	Banking	Increase profitability
Funds raised	Monthly	Internal process	Operations	Charity	Efficient operations
Consent return rate for rework and resubmission (numbers and dollars)	Monthly	Internal process	Planning	Construction	Efficient operations
Measure cost of obtaining planning consents	Quarterly	Internal process	Planning	Construction	Efficient operations
Measure number of projects that do not need special consents (client = cost benefit)	Quarterly	Internal process	Planning	Construction	Efficient operations
Timeliness of resource consents processing	Quarterly	Internal process	Planning	Construction	Efficient operations
Turnaround time of resource consent applications (days elapsed)	Monthly	Internal process	Planning	Construction	Efficient operations
Emergency response time	Weekly	Internal process	Operations	Critical services sector	Efficient operations
Claims frequency	Monthly	Internal process	Accounting	Insurance	Increase profitability

(continues)

Name of Measure	Frequency of Measure	BSC Perspective	Applicable BSC Teams	Applicable Sectors	Strategic Objective
Claims severity	Monthly	Internal process	Accounting	Insurance	Efficient operations
Insurance premiums received from new product launches	Quarterly	Internal process	Sales and Marketing	Insurance	Increase profitability
Accomplishment of quality improvement implementation milestones	Monthly	Internal process	QA	Manufacturing	Efficient operations
Design cycle time	Monthly	Internal process	R&D	Manufacturing	Increase profitability
Downtime due to different types of equipment failure	Weekly	Internal process	Production control, IT	Manufacturing	Efficient operations
Engineering changes to off-the-shelf system by reason	Monthly	Internal process	R&D	Manufacturing	Increase profitability
Engineering changes after design completion	Monthly	Internal process	R&D	Manufacturing	Increase profitability
Improvement in productivity (%)	Monthly	Internal process	Production	Manufacturing	Increase profitability
Number of improvements to products in month	Monthly	Internal process	R&D	Manufacturing	Increase profitability
Inventory system accuracy rates	Monthly	Internal process	Production	Manufacturing	Increase profitability
Inventory turnover (number)	Monthly	Internal process	Production	Manufacturing	Increase profitability
Late items as a percentage of average daily production	Weekly	Internal process	Production	Manufacturing	Efficient operations
Process part-per-million defect rates	Monthly	Internal process	Production	Manufacturing	Efficient operations

Processes made foolproof	Quarterly	Internal process	Production	Manufacturing	Increase profitability
Processes under statistical control with sufficient capability	Quarterly	Internal process	Production	Manufacturing	Increase profitability
Production schedule delays because of material shortages	Weekly	Internal process	Production	Manufacturing	Increase profitability
Production set-up/changeover time	Monthly	Internal process	Production	Manufacturing	Increase profitability
Quality problems attributable to design	Monthly	Internal process	R&D	Manufacturing	Increase profitability
Reduction of parts count on products	Quarterly	Internal process	R&D	Manufacturing	Increase profitability
Service factor—percent of orders filled	Monthly	Internal process	Production	Manufacturing	Increase profitability
Technical support costs/unit sold (quality of product and clarity of instructions)	Weekly	Internal process	QA	Manufacturing	Efficient operations
Time lost due to schedule changes or deviations from schedule	Monthly	Internal process	Production	Manufacturing	Efficient operations
Total value of finished products/total production costs	Weekly	Internal process	Operations	Manufacturing	Increase profitability
Unplanned versus planned maintenance	Monthly	Internal process	Production	Manufacturing	Efficient operations
Waste—all forms: scrap, rejects, underutilized capacity, idle time, downtime, excess production, etc.	Weekly	Internal process	Production	Manufacturing	Increase profitability
Waste caused by maintenance tests	Monthly	Internal process	Production	Manufacturing	Increase profitability
Yield—net good product produced	Weekly	Internal process	Production	Manufacturing	Increase profitability

(continues)

225

Name of Measure	Frequency of Measure	BSC Perspective	Applicable BSC Teams	Applicable Sectors	Strategic Objective
Service calls or complaints per unit sold	Weekly	Internal process	QA	Retail	Increase profitability
Space productivity—sales or production per square foot	Monthly	Internal process	Sales and marketing	Retail	Increase profitability
Number of leads generated by agents	Monthly	Internal process	Sales and marketing	Service	Increase profitability
Reporting errors (e.g., time charged to closed/wrong jobs)	Monthly	Internal process	All teams	Service	Efficient operations
Percentage of bids or proposals accepted	Weekly	Internal process	Sales	Service, manufacturing	Increase profitability
Percentage of customer-facing employees having on-line access to information about customers (effective communication of accurate information to employee)	Monthly	Learning and growth	IT	All sectors	Efficient operations
Percentage of employees below age of X	Quarterly	Learning and growth	HR	All sectors	Skilled and experienced workforce
Percentage of employees who have interacted with customers	Monthly	Learning and growth	HR	All sectors	Skilled and experienced workforce
Percentage of employees with tertiary education	Quarterly	Learning and growth	HR	All sectors	Skilled and experienced workforce
Percentage of managers with satisfactory IT literacy	Monthly	Learning and growth	IT	All sectors	Skilled and experienced workforce
Percentage of new staff (less than three employees) who have had post-employment interview	Monthly	Learning and growth	HR	All sectors	Skilled and experienced workforce

226

Measure	Frequency	Perspective	Owner	Sector	Objective
Percentage of performance reviews completed on time	Monthly	Learning and growth	All teams	All sectors	Efficient operations
Percentage of rising stars with mentors	Quarterly	Learning and growth	HR	All sectors	Skilled and experienced workforce
Percentage of staff performance reviews completed	Monthly	Learning and growth	HR, all teams	All sectors	Skilled and experienced workforce
Percentage of contractors to total staff	Quarterly	Learning and growth	HR	All sectors	Skilled and experienced workforce
Annual rolling average of days training by key team	Monthly	Learning and growth	All teams	All sectors	Skilled and experienced workforce
Average employee years of service with company	Quarterly	Learning and growth	HR	All sectors	Desirable place to work
Closing the skills matrix gap progress	After the performance review round	Learning and growth	HR	All sectors	Skilled and experienced workforce
Competence development expense/payroll cost	Quarterly	Learning and growth	HR	All sectors	Efficient operations
Employees certified for skilled job functions or positions	Quarterly	Learning and growth	HR	All sectors	Skilled and experienced workforce
Employees complying with their development plan	Quarterly	Learning and growth	HR, training	All sectors	Skilled and experienced workforce
Employees terminated for performance, other problems	Monthly	Learning and growth	HR	All sectors	Skilled and experienced workforce
Employees that have improved skills during last six months	Six monthly	Learning and growth	HR, training	All sectors	Skilled and experienced workforce
Employees with delegated spending authority	Quarterly	Learning and growth	HR	All sectors	Skilled and experienced workforce

(continues)

227

Name of Measure	Frequency of Measure	BSC Perspective	Applicable BSC Teams	Applicable Sectors	Strategic Objective
Increase in average grade level of reading and math skills of employees	Quarterly	Learning and growth	HR, training	All sectors	Skilled and experienced workforce
Investment in new product support and training ($)	Quarterly	Learning and growth	Sales	All sectors	Skilled and experienced workforce
Leadership index (based on responses from a section in the employee survey)	Every employee survey (three to four times a year)	Learning and growth	HR	All sectors	Efficient operations
Leadership initiatives targeted to rising stars	Monthly	Learning and growth	HR	All sectors	Skilled and experienced workforce
Managers who have had performance management training	Monthly	Learning and growth	HR	All sectors	Skilled and experienced workforce
Motivation index (based on responses from a section in the employee survey)	Every employee survey (three to four times a year)	Learning and growth	HR	All sectors	Efficient operations
Needs assessment gap—required versus actual skills for positions	Quarterly	Learning and growth	HR, training	All sectors	Skilled and experienced workforce
Number of cumulative work experience (years) in current management team	Quarterly	Learning and growth	HR	All sectors	Skilled and experienced workforce
Number of current users of X system	Quarterly	Learning and growth	IT, HR	All sectors	Skilled and experienced workforce

228

Number of in-house training courses	Quarterly	Learning and growth	HR	All sectors	Skilled and experienced workforce
Number of initiatives implemented from the staff survey	Weekly after the employee survey	Learning and growth	HR	All sectors	Skilled and experienced workforce
Number of internal promotions	Monthly	Learning and growth	HR	All sectors	Skilled and experienced workforce
Number of staff who have agreed to development plans	After the performance review round	Learning and growth	HR	All sectors	Skilled and experienced workforce
Number of teams with a balanced scorecard (BSC)—rollout of a BSC system	Monthly	Learning and growth	Balanced scorecard team	All sectors	Efficient operations
Number of training hours—in both external/internal courses	Monthly	Learning and growth	HR	All sectors	Skilled and experienced workforce
Number of full time temporary employees (contractors over three months)	Quarterly	Learning and growth	HR	All sectors	Skilled and experienced workforce
Number of internal applications for job applications closed in month	Monthly	Learning and growth	HR	All sectors	Skilled and experienced workforce
Number of level 1 and 2 managers who were promoted internally	Quarterly	Learning and growth	HR	All sectors	Skilled and experienced workforce
Number of mentoring meetings by each high performer (rising star)	Quarterly	Learning and growth	HR	All sectors	Skilled and experienced workforce
Number of new staff (less than three months) who attended an induction program	Monthly	Learning and growth	HR	All sectors	Skilled and experienced workforce

(continues)

229

Name of Measure	Frequency of Measure	BSC Perspective	Applicable BSC Teams	Applicable Sectors	Strategic Objective
Number of staff who have attended an induction within four weeks of starting	Monthly	Learning and growth	HR	All sectors	Skilled and experienced workforce
Percentage of managers who are women	Quarterly	Learning and growth	HR	All sectors	Skilled and experienced workforce
Participation in team meetings (% of total team)	Monthly	Learning and growth	All teams	All sectors	Skilled and experienced workforce
Percentage of cross-trained personnel	Quarterly	Learning and growth	Production control, training	All sectors	Skilled and experienced workforce
Number post project reviews undertaken to ascertain lessons learned	Monthly	Learning and growth	Accounting	All sectors	Skilled and experienced workforce
Re-skilled employees percentage of workforce requiring re-skilling	From staff survey	Learning and growth	HR	All sectors	Efficient operations
Staff trained to use X system	Quarterly	Learning and growth	IT, HR	All sectors	Skilled and experienced workforce
Staff training attendance	Monthly	Learning and growth	HR	All sectors	Skilled and experienced workforce
Staff who have verbal feedback about performance every month	Quarterly	Learning and growth	HR	All sectors	Skilled and experienced workforce
Number of succession plans for key positions	Quarterly	Learning and growth	HR	All sectors	Skilled and experienced workforce
Number of suggested improvements from employees by department	Quarterly	Learning and growth	HR	All sectors	Skilled and experienced workforce
Suggestions made to suggestions implemented ratio	Quarterly	Learning and growth	HR	All sectors	Innovation

Measure	Frequency	Perspective	Owner	Sector	Objective
Time in training [days/year] (number)	Monthly	Learning and growth	HR	All sectors	Skilled and experienced workforce
Total hours employees spend in mentoring	Quarterly	Learning and growth	All teams, HR	All sectors	Skilled and experienced workforce
Training days this month	Monthly	Learning and growth	HR	All sectors	Skilled and experienced workforce
Training needs outstanding	Quarterly	Learning and growth	HR	All sectors	Skilled and experienced workforce
Turnover of female staff	Quarterly	Learning and growth	HR	All sectors	Desirable place to work
Turnover of staff by ethnicity	Quarterly	Learning and growth	HR	All sectors	Skilled and experienced workforce
Number of staff who are aware of new initiative	Monthly	Learning and growth	HR	All sectors	Efficient operations
Number of teams who have undertaken internal user satisfaction surveys	Monthly	Learning and growth	HR	All sectors	Skilled and experienced workforce
Percentage of staff meeting continuing professional development requirements	Quarterly	Learning and growth	All teams	Professional service firms	Skilled and experienced workforce
Number of research papers generated	Quarterly	Learning and growth	R&D	Tertiary	Skilled and experienced workforce

INDEX